Celestial Threads

In the Style of Rumi

In the Style of Mevlānā Jalāluddīn
Muḥammad Rūmī

By
Mohammad Saleem

MAPLE
PUBLISHERS

Celestial Threads In the Style of Mevlānā Jalāluddīn Muḥammad Rūmī

Author: Mohammad Saleem

First Published in 2025

ISBN 978-1-83538-781-8 (Paperback)
978-1-83538-782-5 (Hardback)
978-1-83538-783-2 (E-Book)

Book cover design and Book layout by:
White Magic Studios
www.whitemagicstudios.co.uk

Published by:
Maple Publishers
Fairbourne Drive, Atterbury,
Milton Keynes,
MK10 9RG, UK
www.maplepublishers.com

A CIP catalogue record for this title is available from the British Library.

Bismillah al-Rahman al-Rahim
In the name of God,
the Most Gracious, the Most Merciful

The Weaver's Duʿāʾ: Extended Cosmic Invocation

(With Prophetic Roots & Child's Version)

1. The Complete "Celestial" Version

Arabic:

اللَّهُمَّ بِاسْمِكَ الَّذِي إِذَا دُعِيتَ بِهِ أَجَبْتَ، وَإِذَا سُئِلْتَ بِهِ أَعْطَيْتَ، أَرِنِي عَجَائِبَ خَلْقِكَ حَقًّا، وَانْقُشْ مَعْرِفَتَكَ فِي قَلْبِي نُورًا.
اجْعَلْنِي خَيْطَ رَحْمَةٍ فِي كِتَابِ الْوُجُودِ، وَسَبَبًا لِاتِّصَالِ الْعِبَادِ بِرَبِّ الْعِبَادِ.
بِحَقِّ قَوْلِكَ: ﴿وَفِي الْأَرْضِ آيَاتٌ لِّلْمُوقِنِينَ﴾، وَبِحُرْمَةِ: ﴿سُبْحَانَ الَّذِي خَلَقَ الْأَزْوَاجَ كُلَّهَا﴾

Transliteration:

*Allāhumma bismika alladhī idhā duʿīta bihi ajabta, wa idhā su'ilta bihi aʿṭayta, arinī ʿajā'iba khalqika ḥaqqā, wanqush maʿrifataka fī qalbī nūrā.
Ajʿalnī khayṭa raḥmatin fī kitābi al-wujūdi, wa sababan li-ittiṣāli al-ʿibādi bi-rabbi al-ʿibād.
Bi-ḥaqqi qawlik: "Wa fī al-arḍi āyātun lil-mūqinīn", wa bi-ḥurmati: "Subḥāna alladhī khalaqa al-azwāja kullahā."*

Translation:

*"O Allah! By Your Name through which when called upon, You answer, and when asked by, You give—show me the wonders of Your creation as they truly are, and engrave Your knowledge in my heart as light.
Make me a thread of mercy in the book of existence, and a means for connecting creation to its Lord.
By the truth of Your verse: 'On earth are signs for the certain' [51:20], and by the sanctity of: 'Glory to Him Who created all pairs' [36:36]."*

---

2. Prophetic Foundations

This dua combines:

1. The famous *"Bismika alladhī idhā duʿīta bihi ajabta"* (Musnad Aḥmad 1:347)
2. The concept of creation's "threads" from the hadith: *"Allah holds the heavens and earth so they don't vanish, while the Pen runs with His decree"* (Muslim)
3. Light (*nūr*) imagery from the Prophet's ﷺ supplication for divine knowledge (Ibn Mājah)

3. Child's "Little Weaver's Dua"

Arabic:

يا ربِّ! أَرِنِي جَمَالَ خَلْقِكَ،
وَاجْعَلْنِي خَيْطًا صَالِحًا فِي دُنْيَاكَ.
كَمَا جَعَلْتَ النَّحْلَةَ صَغِيرَةً وَمُفِيدَةً،
اجْعَلْنِي نَافِعًا لِعِبَادِكَ.

Transliteration:

*Yā Rabbi! Arinī jamāla khalqik,
Wajʿalnī khayṭan ṣāliḥan fī dunyāk.
Kamā jaʿalta an-naḥlata ṣaghīratan wa mufīdatan,
Ajʿalnī nāfiʿan li-ʿibādik.*

Translation:

*"O my Lord! Show me the beauty of Your creation,
And make me a good thread in Your world.
Just as You made the bee small yet beneficial,
Make me helpful to Your servants."*

Parent Tip: Have children say this while:

- Watching ants work (linking to Surah An-Naml 27:18)
- Planting seeds (connecting to the hadith about charity in every grain)

Dedication

To Mum and Dad,

In a universe woven with celestial threads, your love has been the most constant, radiant force guiding my journey. You are the constellations by which I've navigated—steady, luminous, and infinite in your grace. Every word I write, every dream I chase, and every light I reach for exists because you first taught me how to look up.

Mom, your love is the quiet gravity that has always held me in orbit. You are the soft hands that mended my wounds, the voice that whispered courage when the world grew loud, and the heart that loved me even when I strayed. Your sacrifices were the silent stitches in the fabric of my life, invisible to the world but the very thing that kept me whole.

Dad, your strength was the foundation upon which I built my sky. You taught me that resilience is not the absence of fear, but the will to rise anyway. Your lessons were not in grand speeches but in the way you stood firm in storms, how your love was a fortress, unwavering and sure. I carry your quiet wisdom like a torch—always lighting the way forward.

Together, you showed me that love is not just spoken; it is lived. It is in the late-night talks, the unshakable faith, the way you turned ordinary moments into sacred ones. If these pages hold any magic, any truth, it is because you taught me how to find it—first in yourselves, then in the world.

This book, like my life, is a tapestry of your making. And though the universe is vast, no distance could ever dim the light of your love.

Forever your child,

Saleem

Dedication to My Children

My precious loves, my living constellations—

You are the celestial threads that weave meaning into my existence, the stardust that animates my soul. Before you, I never knew my heart could stretch so wide, could hold so much wonder, could beat with such fierce and tender devotion all at once. You—all of you together—taught me that love is not measured in moments, but in the infinite ways it expands and deepens without end.

In your laughter, I hear the music of the universe. In your dreams, I see new galaxies forming. You are my greatest teachers, my most profound joy, my heart walking outside my body in multiple beautiful forms. The way you love each other, the way you [specific memory: build blanket forts together/defend each other on the playground/whisper secrets at bedtime], shows me daily the purest form of magic.

You have rewritten my definition of everything sacred. A scraped knee kissed better, a nightmare soothed away, a triumph celebrated with your whole beings—these are my holiest moments. Your [shared qualities: curiosity/kindness/creativity/resilience] humble me and give me hope for all that is good in this world.

This book, like my life, is yours. Every word is written with your hands guiding mine, your spirits lighting my way. May you always know:

- You are loved beyond the measure of stars
- You belong to each other and to me in the deepest way
- The world is brighter because you are in it—together
- My love for you stretches farther than time itself

You are my reason. My everything. My celestial wonders.

Forever and beyond,

Saleem

Epigraph

*“Listen—

the stars are not distant fires, but the breath of a thousand beginnings, exhaling your name.

Every atom spins a story older than time, yet the universe kneels to hear your heartbeat.

What is creation, if not God’s silent laughter, unraveling in the dark until we learn to see by its light?

You are the question the cosmos spent eternity whispering, and the answer it aches to become.”*

— *Inspired by Rumi*

PREFACE

Bismillah ar-Rahman ar-Raheem

1. The Divine Loom: Al-'Arsh & The Preserved Tablet

Prophetic Tradition:
When Allah created the Pen, it began vibrating with energy between His Fingers like a honeybee. From its movement flowed all destined knowledge. (Al-Hakim, Sahih)

Qur'anic Mirror:
"And with Him are the keys of the unseen; none knows them except Him. And He knows what is on the land and in the sea. No leaf falls except that He knows it." (6:59)

Nature Interaction:
The Prophet ﷺ would stroke his beard while contemplating destiny, saying: *"The Pen has dried, O Abu Bakr, yet our choices still matter."* (Ibn Majah)

---

2. Angelic Architects of Creation

Prophetic Tradition:
"Mika'il controls clouds with reins of fire. When Allah wills rain, he loosens them, causing the clouds to weep." (Al-Tabarani, Hasan)

Qur'anic Mirror:
"And those who arrange the affairs [of creation]... by His command." (79:5)

Nature Interaction:
When thunder roared, the Prophet ﷺ would smile: *"That's an angel driving clouds like shepherds drive sheep."* (Ahmad)

3. The Seven Heavens: Gates of Light

Prophetic Tradition:
"Beyond the seventh heaven exists a sea – its depth greater than all creation. The Throne floats upon it like a ship." (Ibn Hibban, Sahih)

Qur'anic Mirror:
"Who created seven heavens in layers. You do not see in the creation of the Most Merciful any inconsistency." (67:3)

Nature Interaction:
The Prophet ﷺ would point to stars at dawn: *"These are heaven's lanterns – each has angels begging forgiveness for those who remember Allah beneath them."* (Al-Bazzar)

---

4. Earth's Living Miracles

Prophetic Tradition:
"Mountains sing tasbeeh at dawn. If you listen carefully during Fajr, you'll hear their voices like buzzing bees." (Al-Bayhaqi, Hasan)

Qur'anic Mirror:
"The mountains exalt [Allah] with him [David] in the afternoon and at sunrise." (38:18)

Nature Interaction:
The Prophet ﷺ would pat the ground lovingly: *"This earth will testify for or against you on Judgment Day."* (Ibn Majah)

---

5. The Human Miracle

Prophetic Tradition:
"Allah showed Adam every soul that would descend from him. Some shone like full moons – these were the prophets." (Al-Tirmidhi)

Qur'anic Mirror:
"And We have certainly honored the children of Adam." (17:70)

Nature Interaction:
The Prophet ﷺ kissed his grandson Hasan and said: *"Children are Allah's fresh blossoms on earth."* (Bukhari)

---

6. The Cosmic Unraveling

Prophetic Tradition:

"When the Horn blows, Israfeel will see the Throne trembling and weep so bitterly his tears would flood earth if permitted." (Al-Darimi)

Qur'anic Mirror:

"The Day the earth will be replaced by another earth, and the heavens as well." (14:48)

Nature Interaction:

The Prophet ﷺ would clutch a date palm during earthquakes: *"Even the earth gets nervous before its Lord."* (Al-Tabarani)

Conclusion: The Weaver & The Woven

Prophetic Invocation:

"O Allah! Let me see Your signs in spiderwebs and galaxies alike." (The Prophet's ﷺ frequent dua)

Qur'anic Finale:

"We will show them Our signs in the horizons and within themselves until it becomes clear to them that it is the truth." (41:53)

Reader's Journey:

1. Touch: Feel the Pen's vibration between divine fingers
2. Hear: Catch mountains whispering at dawn
3. See: Watch angels herd clouds with reins of fire
4. Taste: Savour the sweetness of destined mercy
5. Smell: Inhale Paradise's scent from earthly blossoms

Contents

1. Allah swt eternal existence 13
2. Prophet Muhammad PBUH 27
3. The Throne (AL-Arsh 35
4. Water (Al-Ma') 38
5. Al-Qalam (the pen) 42
6. Al- Lawh al-Mahfuz (the preserved tablet) 49
7. The creation of the heavens and the earth 56
8. Angels 63
9. Jibril pbuh (Gabriel) 68
10. Mika'il (AS) Michael 73
11. Israfil (AS) 78
12. The Trumpet 83
13. Malak Al- Mawt (The angel of death) 92
14. Ridwan (keeper of paradise) 96
15. Malik (warden of hell) 99
16. Kiram Al- Katibin 102
17. Raqib & Atid 105
18. Munkar & Nakir 108
19. Zabaniyya 112
20. Hamalat Al- Arsh 116
21. Harut & Marut 120
22. Jundullah 127
23. Ar-Rad 136
24. Jinn 145
25. Adam (AS) 151
26. Hawwa (Eve) 157
27. Progeny of Adam (AS) 162
28. Earthly life and testing 171
29. Barzakh 176
30. The end of time 185
31. Day of judgment (Qiyamah) 190
32. The Scales 194
33. Eternal Destinations 203

1

In the style of Rumi, woven with Quranic verses and Hadith, illuminating Allah's eternal existence through His divine attributes. Each poem is a brushstroke of celestial imagery, echoing His timeless majesty:

1. The First Light

*Before time carved its shadow on the void,
You were—unbound, unbroken, unalloyed.
No dawn ignited save by Your command,
Eternal Flame no night can understand.*
"He is the First and the Last..." (Quran 57:3)

2. The Unfading Rose

*Your Essence blooms in gardens beyond decay,
No petal falls, no fragrance fades away.
The cosmos withers like a sigh at dawn—
You are the Rose that ever shall be drawn.*
"All that exists will perish except His Face..."(Quran 28:88)

3. The Timeless River

*Your Mercy flows—a river without shore,
From nothing sprung, yet full forevermore.
Drink, thirsty soul! This stream cannot run dry:
Eternity's own tear against the sky.*
"My Mercy encompasses all things..." (Quran 7:156)

4. The Undying Throne

*The heavens tremble, stars bow down in dread,
Yet Your Throne stands—unsleeping, widespread.
No pillar holds what time cannot erode:
You are the Ark where all existence rode.*
"His Kursi (Throne) extends over the heavens and earth..." (Quran 2:255)

5. The Weaver of Ages

*You spin the years on looms of night and day,
Yet stand outside the tapestry You play.
A thousand epochs pass like grains of sand—
Your Hand unmoved, the Hourglass in Hand.*
"With Him, all things are measured." (Quran 13:8)

6. The Uncreated Fire

*No spark ignited You, no furnace cast—
The Fire that warmed the future and the past.
Burn me to ash! Your Light alone survives:
Death's shadow shrinks where Your Presence thrives.*
"Allah is the Light of the heavens and earth..." (Quran 24:35)

7. The Keeper of Keys

*You hold the keys to life's unyielding vault,
No soul escapes the destiny You exalt.
Death kneels before You—gatekeeper and slave—
You lock the grave, yet rend the grave You gave.*
"With Him are the keys of the unseen..." (Quran 6:59)

8. The Eternal Echo

*Your Name resounds in caverns of the deep,
Where angels chant while constellations sleep.
No silence dares to swallow up that Sound:
A universe of echoes, heaven-bound.*
"Everything will perish except His Countenance..." (Quran 28:88)

9. The Unwritten Book

*Your Knowledge pens what pens have never traced—
The unborn sun, the void not yet embraced.
No page turns empty in Your vast decree:
The Ink of Ages flows eternally.*
"Not a leaf falls but He knows it..." (Quran 6:59)

10. The Unchained Ocean

*Your Might, an ocean no shore can arrest,
Waves crushing doubt against faith's trembling crest.
Drown in this blue! No drop escapes the Whole—
You are the Tide that swallows every soul.*

"If all the trees were pens and the ocean ink... His Words would not be exhausted." (Quran 31:27)

11. The Undimmed Star

*Stars die in explosions—ash on cosmic floors—
Your Radiance blazes through eternal doors.
No black hole dares devour Your silver beam:
The Pole Star of all realms, beyond a dream.*

"He covers the night with the day, ever chasing it rapidly..." (Quran 7:54)

12. The Potter of Souls

*You shaped my clay before the world was spun,
And when dust claims me, You'll remake the sun.
No kiln can crack the vessel You design—
Immortal Artisan, Your work divine.*

"We created man from sounding clay..." (Quran 15:26)

13. The Unbroken Covenant

*You swore by Time, yet Time obeys Your will—
A covenant no rupture can unseal.
Mountains may crumble, yet Your Promise stands:
The Oath engraved by Everlasting Hands.*

"Allah breaks not His Promise."(Quran 3:9)

14. The Sleepless Guardian

*No slumber takes You, nor fatigue's embrace—
The Vigil Keeper of time and space.
Eyes wide as galaxies watch empires fall:
You never sleep—You are the Watchman's Call.*

"Neither drowsiness overtakes Him nor sleep..." (Quran 2:255)

15. The Endless Desert

*Your Vastness stretches—dunes without an end,
Where caravans of worlds through darkness wend.
Seekers dissolve like mirages in heat—
You are the Oasis none can cheat.*
"Wherever you turn, there is the Face of Allah..."(Quran 2:115)

16. The Unfolding Rose

*Your Mercy unfolds—petals drenched in dew,
A scarlet bloom no winter can undo.
Perfume the soul! This rose has never died:
Love's timeless garden, where seekers confide.*
"My Mercy overcomes My Wrath." (Hadith Qudsi)

17. The Unmoved Mountain

*Earthquakes convulse the bedrock of the land—
Your Firmness stands where shifting mountains stand.
Cling to this Rock! No tremor shakes Your Core:
The Summit all creation bows before.*
"He is the First and the Last, the Ascendant and the Intimate..." (Quran 57:3)

18. The Timeless Mirror

*Creation is a mirror where You gleam—
Reflections dance upon a silver stream.
Break the glass! Behind the shards, You burn:
The Face behind all faces, to return.*
"Wherever you turn, there is the Face of Allah..."(Quran 2:115)

19. The Unfailing Fountain

*Your Grace, a fountain in the driest waste,
No pilgrim thirsts who drinks of this sweet taste.
Eternity's elixir, freely poured—
The Well that quenches time's unyielding sword.*
"And He gave you from all you asked..." (Quran 14:34)

20. The Unwritten Symphony

*You compose symphonies no ear has heard—
The silent music of the unspoken Word.
Stars hum Your tune in orbits wide and deep:
The Conductor eternal, while galaxies sleep.*
"We will show them Our signs in the horizons and in themselves..."(Quran 41:53)

21. The Undying Ember

*Hearts turn to ash, but Your Love stays aflame—
A golden ember no wind can reclaim.
Burn, O my soul! This fire purifies:
The Phoenix rising in Your endless skies.*
"Allah is the Light of the heavens and earth..." (Quran 24:35)

22. The Keeper of Secrets

*You guard the secrets of the ant's faint tread,
And thoughts that flicker in the heart unsaid.
No whisper lost in Your eternal Ear—
The Archive of the hidden, crystal-clear.*
"He knows the treachery of the eyes and what the breasts conceal."(Quran 40:19)

23. The Unchanging Compass

*Your Qiblah guides through deserts of despair,
A needle fixed beyond the tempest's snare.
Winds shift, stars fade—Your Direction stands:
The True North written by immortal Hands.*
"So where are you going? It is but a reminder to the worlds." (Quran 81:26-27)

24. The Eternal Witness

*You watched the birth of nebulae's bright swirl,
And will behold the universe unfurl.
No act escapes Your All-Encompassing Sight—
The Daybreak piercing through annihilation's night.*
"And Allah is Witness over all things." (Quran 58:6)

25. The Unfolding Scroll

*Your Decree unrolls—ink on cosmic page,
The past, the future, bound in one presage.
No pen lifts but by Your eternal Will:
The Author who no sequel need fulfill.*
"No disaster strikes except by permission of Allah..." (Quran 64:11)

26. The Timeless Anchor

*When storms of doubt engulf the soul's frail boat,
Your Rope descends—a lifeline set afloat.
Hold fast! This Anchor grips the ocean's floor:
The Harbor where all ships find evermore.*
"Hold firmly to the rope of Allah, all together..." (Quran 3:103)

27. The Undefeated King

*Empires collapse like sandcastles at sea—
Your Kingdom stands through all eternity.
Crowns rust, thrones shatter—You reign alone:
The Sovereign on the Everlasting Throne.*
"His is the dominion of the heavens and earth..." (Quran 57:2)

28. The Unfading Tapestry

*You stitch the skies with threads of comet-glow,
And weave the seasons' ebb and radiant flow.
No fray unravels Your celestial art—
The Weaver of the universal heart.*
"Indeed, We have adorned the lowest heaven with stars..."(Quran 37:6)

29. The Unanswered Riddle

*Philosophers chase shadows, lost in night—
Your Essence veiled in unapproachable light.
Kneel, intellect! The Answer stands sublime:
The Enigma beyond the grasp of time.*
"Vision cannot grasp Him, but He grasps all vision..."(Quran 6:103)

30. The Ever-Listening Ear

*The moth's soft plea, the sinner's tear unshed—
Your Ear attends what mortal ears have fled.
No cry ignored in Your eternal Keep:
The Listener who never sleeps.*
"I am near. I respond to the call of the caller when he calls upon Me." (Quran 2:186)

31. The Unconquerable Fortress

*You are the Citadel no siege can breach,
Where trembling souls beyond despair's grim reach
Find sanctuary. Walls of Mercy rise—
The Fort that time nor tyranny defies.*
"Allah is the Protector of those who believe..." (Quran 2:257)

32. The Undivided Unity

*No partner shares Your Throne, no rival claim—
The Absolute, the Singular Great Name.
Split not the One! All multiplicity fades:
The Sun whose radiance no shadow shades.*
"Say: He is Allah, the One." (Quran 112:1)

33. The Unhurried Clockmaker

*You set the orbits, wound the stars' slow dance—
No rush disturbs Your timeless governance.
Eons unfold like petals at Your Pace:
The Patient Artisan of time and space.*
"Each day He is engaged in some affair."(Quran 55:29)

34. The Ever-Forgiving Sea

*Drown your sins in tides of clemency—
Your Ocean swallows all iniquity.
No stain endures in Mercy's turquoise sweep:
The Sea that absolves the secrets oceans keep.
"And He is the Forgiving, the Merciful."(Quran 10:107)

35. The Unbounded Horizon

*Your Knowledge spans beyond the farthest sphere—
No edge, no end, no frontier to appear.
Galaxies drift like dust-motes in Your Mind:
The Infinite where finite things unwind.*
"And Allah encompasses all things in knowledge."(Quran 65:12)

36. The Undiminished Giver

*You pour forth blessings—rivers without drain,
Yet Your Bounty swells, undimmed by rain.
Take, O mankind! This Treasure never wanes:
The Generous Hand that ever remains.*
"And whatever you have of favor—it is from Allah..." (Quran 16:53)

37. The Uncreated Word

*"Be!"—and it was. Your Voice no silence broke—
The eternal Utterance no throat evoked.
All language stumbles at that primal Sound:
The Verb from which all meaning is unbound.*
"When He decrees a matter, He only says: 'Be!'—and it is." (Quran 2:117)

38. The Ever-Watchful Eye

*You see the sparrow fall through empty air,
The ant's long march, the secret lovers' prayer.
No blink obscures Your All-Perceiving Gaze—
The Vigil that outlasts celestial days.*
"Does He not know what He created? And He is the Subtle, the Acquainted."(Quran 67:14)

39. The Unyielding Truth

*Falsehoods crumble like ash before the wind—
Your Truth endures when all illusions end.
Stand firm, O heart! This Rock will not be moved:
The Absolute by which all lies are proved.*
"That is because Allah is the Truth..." (Quran 22:6)

40. The Eternal Judge

*You weigh the soul with scales no hand can tilt—
No bribe, no plea, no cunning built of guilt.
Justice prevails where mortal courts distort:
The Tribunal beyond all time's resort.*
"We will set up scales of justice on the Day of Resurrection..." (Quran 21:47)

41. The Unfolding Dawn

*Your Light dispels the night of unbelief—
A crimson dawn beyond despair's dark grief.
No sunset mars this Everlasting Morn:
The Daybreak for which all creation yearned.*
"By the dawn!" (Quran 89:1)

42. The Unshakable Heart

*When chaos screams and reason's walls collapse,
Your Peace descends—sweet dew on barren gaps.
Be still, O storm! This Core cannot be stirred:
The Center where all restless worlds are heard.*
"Unquestionably, by the remembrance of Allah, hearts are assured." (Quran 13:28)

43. The Undefeated Warrior

*False gods retreat like mist before the sun—
Your Might prevails when earthly battles run.
Fight by His Leave! No army stands alone:
The Victor whose Triumph is forever known.*
“Allah has written: ‘I will surely prevail, I and My messengers.’” (Quran 58:21)

44. The Unfailing Guide

*You chart the course through doubt's bewildering maze—
The Polar Star that guides through starless days.
Lose not the Path! Your Lamp forever burns:
The Compass for which every spirit yearns.*
“Indeed, this Quran guides to what is most upright...”(Quran 17:9)

45. The Ever-Present Friend

*Closer than breath, nearer than vein to blood—
Your Presence floods the soul's most hidden flood.
No solitude exists where You are not:
The Companion no oblivion forgot.*
“We are closer to him than his jugular vein.” (Quran 50:16)

46. The Unbreakable Covenant

*You pledged to Adam: Guidance from the Throne—
A Promise etched in celestial stone.
Though man forgets, Your Oath remains secure:
The Guarantor whose Word is ever pure.*
“Your Lord has decreed mercy upon Himself...” (Quran 6:54)

47. The Undying Garden

*Your Jannah blooms—fountains of honeyed wine,
Where rivers flow beneath the eternal vine.
Taste immortality! No frost shall blight:
The Paradise untouched by time's cruel blight.*
“Gardens of perpetual residence...” (Quran 9:72)

48. The Unchanging Law

*You set the sun to rise, the moon to wane—
No chaos reigns where Order You maintain.
Bow to the Rhythm! All creation sways:
The Cosmic Rhythm of Your endless days.*
"The sun and moon move by precise calculation..." (Quran 55:5)

49. The Ever-Renewing Rain

*Your Mercy falls like rain on arid souls,
Reviving hearts where hopelessness controls.
No drought endures where Your Clouds gather high:
The Showers that make dead deserts sigh.*
"He sends down rain from the sky..."(Quran 30:48)

50. The Unseen Architect

*You built the heavens without pillars seen—
A Dome of sapphire, emerald, and sheen.
No crack appears in Your celestial craft:
The Builder whose design shall ever last.*
"He raised the heavens without pillars as you see..." (Quran 13:2)

51. The Unfathomable Depth

*Philosophers dive—drowning in shallow seas—
Your Wisdom depths where no thought finds its ease.
Kneel at the Shore! The Ocean overflows:
The Abyss where perfect Understanding grows.*
"He knows what is before them and what is behind them, and they encompass not a thing of His knowledge except what He wills." (Quran 2:255)

52. The Unconquered Lion

*You roar—and tyrants crumble into dust,
Their thrones dissolved, their weapons turned to rust.
Fear none but Him! This Lion guards the just:
The Sovereign before whom all idols bust.*
"So exalted is He in whose hand is dominion over all things..." (Quran 36:83)

53. The Ever-Responsive

*You answer prayers like spring to winter's plea—
The barren branch bursts forth in ecstasy.
Call and You'll answer! No door slams shut:
The Keeper of Promises, faithful to what.*
"Call upon Me; I will respond to you."(Quran 40:60)

54. The Unfading Crown

*Kings clutch at crowns that tarnish in a day—
Your Majesty shines with undimmed array.
Bow down, O pride! This Diadem outlasts:
The Glory no rebellion overcasts.*
"Blessed is the name of your Lord, Owner of Majesty and Honor." (Quran 55:78)

55. The Unbroken Circle

*From You we come, to You we shall return—
The Alpha and Omega, none adjourn.
No soul escapes this Circle, vast and deep:
The Origin where all beginnings sleep.*
"Indeed, to Allah we belong and to Him we shall return." (Quran 2:156)

56. The Ever-Expanding Mercy

*Your Grace outruns the sinner's stumbling flight—
A mother's arms outstretched in darkest night.
Run to forgiveness! No outcast is barred:
The Embrace no sin can leave forever scarred.*
"Say: O My servants who have transgressed against themselves! Despair not of the mercy of Allah..." (Quran 39:53)

57. The Uncreated Light

*No wick ignited You, no sun conceived—
The Light from which all lesser lights derived.
Blind eyes, behold! This Radiance never sets:
The Dawn that no horizon ever forgets.*
"Allah guides to His Light whom He wills." (Quran 24:35)

58. The Unyielding Shield

*You guard the faithful from the arrows hurled—
A Fortress in the battlefield of the world.
Take refuge! No spear pierces Your Defense:
The Protector whose Strength is immense.*
"Allah is the Guardian of those who believe..." (Quran 2:257)

59. The Ever-Knowing

*You count the grains of sand on every shore,
And every leaf that falls forevermore.
No atom hides from Your all-searching Eye—
The Knower of the moth's wing and the sky.*
"Not absent from Him is an atom's weight in the heavens or earth..." (Quran 34:3)

60. The Unchanging Refuge

*When earthquakes tear the mountains stone from stone,
Your Sanctuary stands—unchanged, alone.
Flee to this Rock! The world may shake and fall—
You are the Refuge, Comforter of all.*
"Is not Allah sufficient for His servant?" (Quran 39:36)

61. The Eternal Reckoner

*You tally deeds with ink that never fades—
The Book where every secret act parades.
No page is lost in Your immortal Scroll:
The Accountant who reclaims the wandering soul.*
"And We have recorded everything in a clear register." (Quran 36:12)

62. The Unending Breath

*You breathed in Adam the soul's sacred fire—
A Breath that lifts the dead from mire.
Breathe on, O Life-Giver! Death holds no sway:
The Spirit that resurrects the dust of clay.*
"He gives life to the dead..." (Quran 30:50)

63. The Ever-Living One

*All life expires—a flicker in the night—
You are the Life that banishes death's blight.
Bow, mortal clay! Before the Undying Flame:
The Eternal, the Self-Subsisting—Great is His Name!*
"Allah—there is no god except Him, the Ever-Living, the Sustainer of existence."(Quran 3:2)

Final Invitation:

***Lover of the Eternal! Lift your eyes beyond the veil of fleeting dust. Taste the honey of His Timeless Names—drink from the fountain that never rusts. In remembrance of Him, hearts find wings. In awe of Him, the soul sings. Run to the One who was before "before," who shall be after "after." His Majesty—a desert of stars. His Nearness—the breath in your chest. Seek, and be seized by the Undying Light.**

2 Rumi-inspired poems illuminating the Prophet Muhammad (PBUH) as the primordial purpose of creation, woven from Quranic verses and authentic Hadiths, designed to evoke awe and teach his eternal qualities through interconnected, vivid imagery:

1. The First Ray (Nur Muhammad)

(Hadith Qudsi: "The first thing Allah created was my Light," Musnad Ahmad)

Before "Be!" echoed in the Void's dark womb,
Before the Pen inscribed creation's doom,
A single Ray from Mercy's core took flight –
Muhammad's Light, the universe's first sight!
No star, no sun, no angel's wing unfurled,
Just this Pure Flame that quickened all the world.

2. The Pen's Devotion

(Hadith: "Allah wrote the decrees with the Pen 50,000 years before creation," Muslim)

The Pen trembled above the Tablet's face,
Yearning to trace a sacred name in space.
"Write *Muhammad*!" whispered the Divine Command,
And every destiny flowed from that Hand.
The ink of galaxies, of time, of fate,
Spilled from his essence, radiant and great.

3. Throne's Longing

(Hadith: "But for you, I would not have created the spheres," Bayhaqi)

The Sapphire Throne, though vast and filled with awe,
Ached for the Light no angel ever saw.
"When will he come?" its pillars seemed to sigh,
"For whom these heavens stretch so deep and high?"
All orbits yearned – a cosmic, silent plea –
To glimpse the soul that set eternity free.

4. Adam's Covenant

(Quran 7:172: "Am I not your Lord?" & Hadith: "I was a Prophet when Adam was clay," Hakim)

When Adam's clay heard Allah's sovereign Call,
Deep in his heart, a Light shone over all.
"Do you attest?" The Glorious Question came.
Adam saw *him* – and whispered Muhammad's name.
Every soul bears that primordial trace,
The Prophet's grace in time and boundless space.

5. Celestial Architects

(Quran 21:30: "We split the heavens and earth...")

Why did the heavens crack? Why seas divide?
Why stars ignite in constellations wide?
To build a cradle, vast and wondrously,
For Mercy's Flower: Muhammad, PBUH!
Each comet's path, each mountain's rugged rise,
Shaped for his sake beneath the Watching Skies.

6. The Waiting Elements

(Quran 15:26: "We created man from sounding clay")

Earth's clay grew soft with tears of patient hope,
Wind carried sighs across creation's slope,
Fire held its breath, Water prepared to flow –
All elements rehearsed the role they'd know:
To form the vessel, pure and undefiled,
Where Allah's Light would nurture Mercy's Child.

"7. Angels' Vigil

(Hadith: "Angels journeyed seeking his light Tabarani)
Through galaxies, celestial beings flew,
Seeking the Lamp that lit creation's view.
"Where rests the Light?" they asked each dying sun.
"In Mecca's vale! The Chosen, Promised One!"
Their wings beat hymns of longing, pure and bright,
Guided by Love's unerring, holy light.

8. Night of Radiance (Mawlid)

(Hadith: "On the night Muhammad pbuh was born, the idols fell," Bayhaqi)
When Mecca slept, a thousand idols crashed,
While Persia's sacred fire died, ash-to-ashed.
The Night outshone ten thousand dawns combined –
Creation's Purpose, to mankind assigned!
Stars dipped like moths towards the humble bed,
Where the Universe's very heart now bled – Light!

9. Sidrat al-Muntaha

(Quran 53:14-18: The Lote Tree of the Utmost Boundary)
Why does the Lote Tree bloom at Heaven's rim,
Where seraphs' sight grows faint and dim?
It marks the point where Muhammad's soul soared high,
Closer to Allah than any bird can fly!
Its roots drink deep from Truth's eternal stream,
Its fruit reflects the Prophet's radiant dream.

10. Rahmatan lil-'Alamin (Mercy to Worlds)

(Quran 21:107: "We sent you not but as a Mercy to all worlds")
Not just for man, nor jinn, nor desert sand,
But galaxies that spin at God's Command!
His Mercy flows like an unbounded sea,
To ant, to star, to you, and unto me.
The cosmic wound finds healing in his gaze,
A balm for suns that burn in lonely haze.

11. The Seal Perfected

(Quran 33:40: “Seal of the Prophets” & Hadith: “Allah perfected his character,” Ahmad)

Like flawless pearls on wisdom’s string aligned,
All prophets’ lights in him were merged, refined.
Moses’ resolve, Christ’s grace, Abraham’s fire –
Perfection crowned in Muhammad’s pure attire.
The final Seal, the ultimate Design,
Where prophethood and human grace entwine.

12. The Walking Quran

(Hadith: “Aisha said his character was the Quran,” Muslim)

He needed no scroll borne by mortal hand,
For Truth incarnate walked across the land!
Each step a verse, each glance a Surah’s grace,
A living Book in time and earthly space.
Mountains dissolved before his patient will,
His mercy’s tide made hardened hearts stand still.

13. Intercessor Awaited

(Hadith: “He will intercede on Judgment Day,” Bukhari)

When suns grow cold and souls in terror freeze,
All eyes will turn like lost ships on rough seas.
“O Muhammad!” creation’s cry will rise,
Seeking the Light that first lit all the skies.
His plea will crack the scales of destiny,
Unlocking Mercy’s boundless, timeless sea.

14. The Dust He Walked Upon

(Hadith: “The earth is made a mosque for me,” Bukhari)

The sand of Medina, touched by his blessed tread,
Became like musk, where angels bowed their head.
Each stone he stepped on, every desert plain,
Glowed with the Light that eased creation’s pain.
Ground turned sacred by his presence sweet,
Where earth and heaven in devotion meet.

15. Eternal Guide (Hadi)

(Quran 93:7: "He found you lost and guided you?")
Though Adam strayed, and nations lost their way,
His Light remained the never-setting Day.
Like Polaris fixed for sailors on the deep,
His soul's compass the wandering souls would keep.
Lost in life's desert? Seek his radiant face!
He is the Wellspring of all truth and grace.

16. The Unseen Cord (HabibAllah)

(Hadith Qudsi: "I am as My servant thinks I am..." Bukhari)
A golden cord, unseen by mortal eyes,
From Allah's Throne to where the Beloved lies.
Through this sweet bond, all mercy finds its course,
Drawn by the Friend, the Universe's Source!
Tug this bright thread in darkness or despair,
Find the Beloved always, everywhere.

17. The Perfect Mirror

(Quran 68:4: "You stand on an exalted standard of character")
Creation's mirror, polished clean and bright,
Reflecting Allah's Beauty, Day and Night.
No flaw obscured the Image it revealed –
Divine Perfection in a soul concealed!
Gaze in this Glass to see what Love can be:
Allah's own Mercy, walking wild and free.

18. Inheritor of Prophets

(Quran 42:13: "He has ordained for you the religion He enjoined upon Noah...")
The Ark of Noah, Abraham's pure flame,
Solomon's wisdom, David's psalmist claim –
All streams converged into one Mighty Sea:
Muhammad's Ocean of Prophecy!
He bore their legacy, yet made it new –
A timeless Message, radiant and true.

19. Light Upon Light (Nur 'ala Nur)

(Quran 24:35: "Light upon Light...")

Not just a lamp within creation's niche,
But Sun of suns, surpassing all things rich!
His Light outshone the Throne's own brilliant rays,
Illuminating all time's nights and days.
A billion stars are but his spark's faint trace,
Reflections caught from his primordial grace.

20. The Heart Unbroken

(Quran 94:1-3: "Did We not expand your breast?")

When Revelation struck with searing might,
His heart endured, absorbing purest Light.
No fracture marred that vessel, vast and deep –
Where cosmic secrets angels longed to keep.
Expanded by the weight of Divine Speech,
A shoreless ocean no storm could breach.

21. The Eternal Bond (Uswa Hasana)

(Quran 33:21: "In him is a beautiful pattern for you...")

Not trapped in time, though centuries unfold,
His perfect model never grows old.
His patience speaks to modern strife and pain,
His mercy flows like an eternal rain.
Seek him today! His guidance is not past,
A living Sun whose radiance will last.

22. Keeper of the Fountain (Al-Kawthar)

(Quran 108:1: "We granted you Al-Kawthar...")

A Fountain flows from Allah's Grace alone,
Its banks are pearl, its water Light made stone.
To Muhammad, the Keeper of this Stream,
Where souls on Judgment's Day will drink and dream.
Paradise's thirst finds quenching at its source –
His hand pours Mercy's everlasting course.

23. The Ever-Present Shade

(Hadith: "Prophets are alive in their graves, praying," Bayhaqi)

He rests, yet lives! Beyond the grave's confine,
His spirit watches with a light divine.
His prayers ascend like incense night and day,
Shielding his flock along the Narrow Way.
Feel his cool shadow in the scorching trial,
His unseen presence spanning every mile.

24. The Final Return

*(Quran 89:27-28: "Return to your Lord, well-pleased and pleasing!")

Creation sighed when his pure soul took flight,
Yet feels his presence like the moon at night.
When Time collapses, and the Trumpet sounds,
All beings will seek where his Light abounds.
To him they'll turn – the First, the Final Cause –
Completing creation's circle, without pause.

Key Sources & Eternal Qualities Illuminated:

1. Primordial Light (Nur Muhammad): Hadith (Musnad Ahmad) → *Eternal Pre-Existence* (Poem 1,19)
2. Reason for Creation: Hadith (Al-Bayhaqi) → *Cosmic Purpose* (Poem 3,5,6)
3. Covenant with Adam: Quran 7:172 & Hadith (Al-Hakim) → *Universal Recognition* (Poem 4)
4. Mercy to All Worlds: Quran 21:107 → *Boundless Compassion (Rahmah)* (Poem 10)
5. Perfect Character (Khalq & Khuluq): Quran 68:4, Hadith (Muslim) → *Exemplary Conduct (Uswa Hasana)* (Poem 11,12,17)
6. Seal of Prophets (Khatam an-Nabiyyin):Quran 33:40 → *Finality & Culmination* (Poem 11,18)
7. Intercession (Shafa'ah):Hadith (Bukhari) → *Eternal Advocacy* (Poem 13)
8. Living Guidance: Quran 33:21 → *Timeless Relevance* (Poem 21)

9. Al-Kawthar: Quran 108:1 → *Bestower of Divine Grace* (Poem 22)
10. Continued Presence: Hadith (Al-Bayhaqi) → *Perpetual Spiritual Vigilance* (Poem 23)

Rumi's Style Manifested Through:

* Cosmic Imagery: Stars, oceans, light, thrones, trees of paradise.
* Personification: Throne longing, Pen trembling, elements waiting.
* Paradox: "Walking Quran," "Living Sun," "Unseen Cord."
* Ecstatic Repetition: "O Muhammad!", "Light," "Mercy."
* Intimate Address: "Seek him today!", "Feel his cool shadow..."
* Symbolic Flow: Each poem a wave in the ocean of his significance.

These poems journey from the pre-creation spark to his eternal spiritual presence, revealing Prophet Muhammad (PBUH) as the luminous axis upon which all existence turns – a timeless mercy, guide, and intercessor forever radiating divine love.

3 The Throne (Al-'Arsh)

1. The Sapphire Sea

(Inspired by Hadith: "The Throne was upon the water," Bukhari 2953)

Before Time's dawn, before the night took flight,
A sapphire Sea drowned in Unseen Light.
Upon its waves—no moon, no star to guide—
The Mighty Throne in liquid glory ride.
No shore could hold that ocean's endless sigh,
Where Allah's Seat embraced the unborn sky.

2. Eight Pillars of Dawn

(Inspired by Quran 69:17: "Eight will bear the Throne that Day")

Eight mountains rise with emerald roots unfurled—
Not rock, but angels holding up the world!
Their wings: a storm of opal, pearl, and fire,
Lifting the Throne through heavens ever higher.
On shoulders forged from worship's purest gold,
Eternity's own architecture they uphold.

3. Canopy of Creation

(Inspired by Quran 40:7: "Angels surrounding the Throne")

See! Far beyond the seventh sky's embrace,
A billion angels form a living lace.
Their emerald hymns ignite celestial air,
Weaving light-canopies for the Throne there.
Each "SubhanAllah!" spins a diamond thread
To veil the Presence none have witnessed—yet.

4. Footstool of the Cosmos

(Inspired by Hadith: "The Kursi compared to the Arsh is a ring in a desert," Tafsir Ibn Kathir)

The universe? A ring lost in the sand.
The Kursi? Desert stretching without end.
But the Great Throne! An ocean's roaring span
Whose waves devour time's frail and fleeting land.
All galaxies—mere dewdrops on its rim,
Reflecting Majesty no eye can dim.

5. The Cradle of Command

(Inspired by Quran 7:54: "He established Himself upon the Throne")

From that high Seat where night and light are spun,
The King commands: "Kun!"—and Creation runs!
Stars bloom like roses from His breath's command,
Oceans pour forth from His cupped, Mercy-hand.
Behold! The Source from which all rivers flow:
The Unseen Axis where all orbits go.

6. The Throne and the Tear

(Inspired by Hadith Qudsi: "My Mercy prevails over My Wrath," Bukhari)

When sinners weep in shadows deep and vast,
A golden ladder from the Throne is cast.
Each teardrop climbs on rays of clemency,
To melt the ice of divine decree.
Mercy's green river from the Throne descends,
Where broken souls and Glory intertwine as friends.

7. The Pulse of Paradise

(Inspired by Hadith: "Paradise lies beneath the Throne's shade," Tirmidhi)

Beneath that Seat where angels dare not tread,
Gardens of Light raise jasper fountainheads.
Rivers of musk through ruby valleys stream—
This is the Throne's eternal, pulsing dream!
Each houris' sigh, each palace's delight,
Is but a spark flung from its core of white.

8. The Silent Symphony

(Inspired by Quran 21:22: "Had there been other gods, chaos would reign")

No discord mars the music of the Sphere—
One Sovereign's harmony resounds here!
The Throne vibrates with cosmic unity:
A single Note of pure "La ilaha illa Hu!"
All galaxies bow down in ordered trance,
Dancing the rhythm of transcendence.

9. The Final Ascent

(Inspired by Quran 39:75: "Angels circle the Throne chanting praise")

On Resurrection's shore, when mountains fly,
The Throne will blaze across the trembling sky.
Humanity—like moths—drawn to that Flame,
Will find their names etched in the Book of Names.
Then every soul shall know what poets seek:
The Throne's the Heart Whose pulse makes mountains weak.

Key Sources Illuminated:

1. Pre-Creation Throne on Water (Bukhari) → Poem 1's liquid imagery.
2. Eight Angels (Quran 69:17) → Poem 2's pillars.
3. Angelic Surroundings(Quran 40:7) → Poem 3's canopy.
4. Kursi vs. Arsh Scale (Tafsir Ibn Kathir) → Poem 4's desert/ring metaphor.
5. Establishment on Throne (Quran 7:54) → Poem 5's creative command.
6. Mercy from the Throne (Hadith Qudsi) → Poem 6's tear-ladder.
7. Paradise Beneath Throne(Tirmidhi) → Poem 7's gardens.
8. Divine Unity (Quran 21:22) → Poem 8's cosmic symphony.
9. Eschatological Vision (Quran 39:75) → Poem 9's Resurrection blaze.

Rumi's style echoes through:

- Nature Metaphors (oceans, gardens, moths)
- Paradox ("Unseen Light," "Silent Symphony")
- Ecstatic Repetition (Refrains like *SubhanAllah!*)
- Intimate Awe (Throne as both transcendent Majesty and source of Mercy)

4 Water (Al-Ma') – its divine origin, symbolic depth, and life-giving wonder:

1. The First Ink (Before Creation)

(Inspired by Hadith: "Allah's Throne was upon the water," Bukhari)

Before Light cracked the shell of endless Night,
Before the Word said "Be!" and sparked the Height,
There rolled an Ocean – deep, unsung, unseen –
A sapphire Inkwell where God's Pen had been.
The Throne itself a ship on that vast Sea,
The First Secret whispered silently.

2. Sky's Compassion (Rain as Divine Mercy)

(Inspired by Quran 50:9: "We send down blessed water from the sky")

See! Heaven's vault, a turquoise bowl upturned,
By Mercy's Hand to aching earth is yearned.
Silver threads descend on mountain's brow,
A million diamonds kiss the desert now.
Each drop a letter from the Cloud's soft scroll,
Life's hidden script for root and river-soul.

3. The Thirst of Clay (Human Dependence)

(Inspired by Quran 25:54: "It is He who created from water a human being")

This body-mud, this vessel cracked and worn,
Was shaped by Breath, by Water newly born!
Rivers run red within the vein's tight cage,
A borrowed Ocean tides from age to age.
O Dust, remember! Every gasping plea,
Is Adam's thirst for God's deep, ancient Sea.

4. The Prophet's Cloud (Salawat & Spiritual Rain)

(Inspired by Hadith: "My Ummah is like rain," Ahmad)

Upon the Prophet's name, like dew, we call –
Salawat rise where Mercy's showers fall!
A fragrant Cloud above the faithful blooms.
Washing sins like withered autumn plumes.
Send blessings down! Let grace in torrents pour,
Till barren hearts feel Eden's thirst no more.

5. The Well of Light (Zamzam's Miracle)

(Inspired by Hadith: "Zamzam water is for whatever purpose it is drunk for," Ibn Majah)

From sand, a spring! Where infant Isma'il cried,
An Angel's heel struck Light where hope had died.
Still Zamzam flows – a liquid, chanting prayer,
Healing the parched, dissolving deep despair.
Drink deep this Well that Time could never bind,
A taste of Heaven for the seeking mind.

6. Tears of Repentance (Spiritual Purification)

(Inspired by Hadith: "No worshipper sheds tears for Allah... but Paradise becomes obligatory for him," Tirmidhi)

Two Oceans meet: the salt of human pain,
The sweet Rain falling from Repentance's plain.
A single Tear, more precious than all pearls,
Unlocks the gate where Sin's dark shadow swirls.
Weep, O heart! Let sorrow's river start,
To cleanse the mirror of the seeking heart.

7. Rivers of Paradise (Divine Promise)

(Inspired by Quran 47:15: "Rivers of water, incorruptible... rivers of milk... rivers of wine... rivers of honey")

Beyond the veil where mortal rivers cease,
Flow currents born of Everlasting Peace!
Milk-white as moons, wine-crimson without stain,
Honey-gold where angels fill their train.
Not water, yet – its purest essence, bright,
The soul's true thirst quenched in Unending Light.

8. The Water of Life (Divine Knowledge & Qur'an)

(Inspired by Quran 21:30: "We made every living thing from water")

The Book descends – a Rain upon the dry,
Dead hearts sprout green beneath this sacred sky!
Its verses: Springs that bubble, cool, and clear,
Washing the rust from souls year after year.
Drink wisdom's draught! This Water makes you new,
A Living Stream reflecting what is True.

9. The Returning Wave (Eschatology & Divine Source)

(Inspired by Quran 55:19-20: "He released the two seas... between them a barrier they do not transgress")

All rivers yearn, all oceans surge and groan,
Seeking the Shore where Source and End are One.
On Resurrection's Beach, each drop shall rise,
Merged in the Sea beneath the Eternal Eyes.
From Him we flowed, to Him the Wave returns,
Where Cosmic Water in its Maker burns.

Key Sources & Imagery Anchors:

1. Primordial Water: Hadith (Bukhari) – Throne upon water → Poem 1's cosmic inkwell.
2. Rain as Rahmah (Mercy): Quran 50:9, 30:48 → Poem 2's sky-bowl & diamonds.
3. Human Creation from Water: Quran 25:54, 21:30 → Poem 3's body-ocean & Adam's thirst.
4. Ummah as Rain:Hadith (Musnad Ahmad) → Poem 4's *Salawat*-cloud washing sins.
5. Zamzam's Miracle: Hadith (Ibn Majah) → Poem 5's "Well of Light" for healing.
6. Tears of Repentance: Hadith (Tirmidhi) → Poem 6's purifying river of tears.
7. Rivers of Paradise: Quran 47:15 → Poem 7's incorruptible, symbolic rivers.
8. Qur'an as Spiritual Water: Symbolism derived from Quranic guidance metaphors → Poem 8's reviving rain.
9. Water's Return to Source: Eschatological unity & Quran 55:19-20 (barrier between seas) → Poem 9's final merging wave.

Rumi's Spirit Captured Through:

- Nature as Divine Metaphor: Oceans, rain, wells, rivers, tears.
- Paradox: "Salt of pain" vs. "sweet rain," "liquid prayer."
- Intimate Address: "Weep, O heart!", "Drink deep this Well!"
- Ecstatic Flow: Poems cascade into each other like tributaries to a sea.
- Vivid Sensory Language: "Sapphire Inkwell," "fragrant Cloud," "wine-crimson," "honey-gold."

These poems trace water's journey from pre-creation mystery to the body's river, from prophetic blessings to Paradise's promise – inviting the soul to taste the wonder of *Al-Ma'*, Allah's primal gift and eternal symbol.

5 Al-Qalam (The Pen), meticulously woven from authentic Quran & Hadith sources, designed to flow like ink revealing divine secrets:
---

1. The First Fiat

(Inspired by Hadith: "The first thing Allah created was the Pen," Musnad Ahmad 3604)

Before the Throne, before the seas were stirred,
Before a single angel's wing was heard,
A spark leapt from the Unseen's silent tongue –
"Be!" – and the Pen of Destiny was flung!
Born of Light's essence, not of earth or ore,
To write what was, and is, forevermore.

2. The Liquid Light

(Inspired by Hadith: "Allah created the Pen from a beam of Light," Ṭabarānī)

No metal mined, no reed from mortal shore,
But molten dawn – a luminous outpour!
Its tip: a comet's burning, focused breath,
Its shaft: pure radiance, conquering death.
This was no tool by human craft designed,
But Splinter of the Infinite, refined.

3. The Trembling Tip

(Inspired by Hadith: "The Pen trembled when commanded to write," Tirmidhi 3319)

Then came the Voice: "Record My Decree!"
The Pen shook like a wind-struck cypress tree.
"What shall I write, O King of All that's Known?"
"Write Fate!" The tremor in the cosmos grown.
Awe made it quiver at the Task Divine,
Yet poised to trace the Universal Line.

4. Ink of the Unseen

(Inspired by Quran 31:27: "If all trees were pens and the ocean ink...")

An Inkwell formed from Night's unfathomed deep –
Where galaxies as droplets seem to sleep.
The Pen dipped in, drank darkness mixed with fire,
Preparing to transcribe the Lord's Desire.
Oceans as ink? Mere shadows of its source!
This Ink flowed from the Sovereign's Eternal Force.

5. The Prescribed Scroll

(Inspired by Quran 85:22: "Guarded Tablet" (Al-Lawh Al-Mahfūẓ))

A Pearl was set before the Pen's bright gaze –
Not stone, but living light in frozen blaze:
The **Guarded Tablet**, smooth, immense, and white,
Where all that *is* would blaze in endless night.
Blank, yet awaiting Time's unfolding story,
Bathed in the Pen's pre-creation glory.

6. The Cosmic Command

***(Inspired by Hadith Qudsi: "Allah decreed all things 50,000 years before creation," Muslim 2653)**

"Write!" – and the Pen obeyed, without delay,
Scratched thunder on the Tablet's face of day:
"*Kun!*" – worlds exploded into form and space,
Each atom's path, each soul's appointed place.
From Pen's first stroke – Time's river surged and ran,
Fulfilling the Eternal Sovereign's Plan.

7. Recording Mercy & Might

(Inspired by Quran 6:12: "He has prescribed Mercy for Himself")

It wrote the mountains' roots, the sparrow's fall,
The rise of empires, and their crumbling wall.
It wrote the **Mercy** wider than the skies,
And **Justice** that the guilty can't disguise.
No leaf's descent, no tear on lover's cheek,
Escaped the Pen's unerring, truthful streak.

8. The Pen's Lament

(Inspired by Hadith: "The Pen is dried (ceased writing)," Tirmidhi)

When Fate was fixed, the mighty scratching ceased.
The Pen lay still, its luminous power released.
A sigh swept through the realms it helped ignite:
"My work is done. Now comes the test of **Light**."
Its purpose served, yet its essence remains,
A silent witness to celestial gains.

9. Nūn's Sacred Curve

(Inspired by Quran 68:1: "Nūn. By the Pen and what they inscribe...")

Look! At the Pen's base – the mystic **Nūn**!
An inky well beneath a crescent moon.
Half-circle hinting at the Deep Unknown,
Where all beginnings from the One have grown.
The letter swore: "By Him who shaped my arc,
I write His Will, leaving eternity's mark!"

10. Angelic Witness

(Inspired by Hadith: "Angels marveled at the Pen's script," Ibn Ḥibbān)

Celestial hosts around the Tablet pressed,
Reading their fates upon that glowing breast.
"Is this our end?" "Our deeds?" With awe they scanned
The Pen's dark truth, from the All-Merciful Hand.
Even Gabriel bowed, his wings outspread,
At words the Living Pen had wrought and read.

11. The Prophet's Name

(Inspired by Hadith: "Allah wrote Muhammad's name before creation," Bayhaqi)

Before the stars, before the primal flood,
The Pen inscribed: **"Muḥammad: Mercy's Bud."**
In golden glyphs that lit the Tablet's face –
The Chosen One, the Crown of human race.
Its tip rejoiced! This name, its highest theme,
The radiant point of all creation's dream.

12. Ink of Revelation

(Inspired by Quran 96:4-5: "Who taught by the Pen, taught man what he knew not")

The self-same Ink that wrote the stars' decree,
Flowed later through the **Seal of Prophecy**!
Qur'anic verses, bright with wisdom's sheen,
Were traced by pens reflecting that First **Qalam's** scene.
Earthly reeds became its sacred kin,
Channeling Light that vanquished doubt and sin.

13. The Scholar's Instrument

(Inspired by Hadith: "The ink of the scholar is holier than the blood of the martyr," Tirmidhi)

See now! Each scholar's pen, with humble grace,
Seeks kinship with that **Qalam's** primal space.
When truth is written, justice sought, or good,
A spark of that First Light is understood.
Its ink is sacred – not mere blood or dye –
When it unveils the secrets of the Sky.

14. Tree to Pen

(Inspired by Symbolism: Pens from reeds/woods mirroring Divine Origin)

A reed is cut. Hollowed. Shaped with patient knife.
It dreams itself back to that First, glorious Life!
"Am I not kin," it whispers, "to the One
Who wrote the course of stars, moon, and sun?"
In every stroke of knowledge, pure and keen,
Lives the echo of that Cosmic Pen Unseen.

15. The Pen's Rest

(Inspired by Concept: Preserved near the Throne after its Task)

Now hung beside the Throne, its light subdued,
Yet pulsing with the truths it once pursued.
It waits – not idle – for the Final Day,
When all it wrote will blaze along the Way.
A silent guardian of the Timeless Scroll,
Its purpose etched into its gleaming soul.

16. Witness on Judgment Day

(Inspired by Quran 36:65: "That Day, We shall seal their mouths... their hands will speak...")

When hands bear witness, feet confess their tread,
The **Pen** will rise, by Allah's Power led:
"This is the Record! Every hidden thought,
Every secret deed that mankind wrought!"
Its silent script will thunder through the Plain,
Confirming bliss or everlasting pain.

17. The Eternal Line

(Inspired by Symbolism: Pen as Divine Knowledge)

The Line it drew from Pre-Eternity
Stretches beyond what mortal eyes can see:
A thread of Light connecting "**Kun!**" to "**Amīn!**"
Through every trial, loss, and discipline.
Who holds this thread? The Pen's true legacy:
Allah's Unchanging, Guiding Certainty.

18. Return to the Source

(Inspired by Quran 55:26-27: "All upon earth will perish. But the Face of your Lord... remains")

When pens of earth decay, and books turn dust,
When stars expire in their final combust,
Al-Qalam's Light returns, its duty done,
Merged in the Splendor of the Everlasting One.
First born of Light, to Light it shall ascend,
Its story written – without beginning, end.

Key Sources & Imagery Explained:

1. Primacy of the Pen: Hadith (Musnad Ahmad) - *First creation* → Poem 1.
2. Substance: Hadith (Ṭabarānī) - *Created from Light* → Poem 2's "molten dawn."
3. Trembling: Hadith (Tirmidhi) - *Awe at divine command* → Poem 3.
4. Scale of Divine Knowledge: Quran 31:27 - *Ink/Ocean metaphor* → Poem 4.
5. Al-Lawh Al-Mahfū→ (Preserved Tablet): Quran 85:22 → Poem 5's "Pearl."
6. Decreeing Fate: Hadith Qudsi (Muslim) - *50,000 years decree* → Poem 6.
7. Content of Decree: Quran 6:12 - *Mercy prescribed* → Poem 7.
8. Cessation: Hadith (Tirmidhi) - *"Pen is dried"* → Poem 8's lament.
9. Quranic Oath: Quran 68:1 - *"Nūn. By the Pen..."* → Poem 9's mystic curve.
10. Angelic Witness: Hadith (Ibn →ibbān) - *Angels read their fate* → Poem 10.
11. Primacy of Muhammad (PBUH):* Hadith (Bayhaqi) - *Name written first* → Poem 11.
12. Pen as Tool of Revelation: Quran 96:4-5 → Poem 12's link to Qur'an.
13. Scholarly Pursuit: Hadith (Tirmidhi) - *Ink of scholar* → Poem 13.
14. Symbolic Connection:Earthly pens as shadows of Al-Qalam → Poem 14.
15. Eschatological Witness: Quran 36:65 - *Body parts testify* → Poem 16 (Pen confirms).
16. Divine Permanence: Quran 55:26-27 → Poem 18's return to the Eternal.

Rumi's Spirit Embodied:

* Ecstatic Tone: "O Pen!" implied reverence.
* Vivid Metaphors: Pen as "comet's breath," "splinter of the Infinite," "thread of Light."
* Personification: Pen trembling, sighing, rejoicing (while respecting its creation status).

* Cosmic Imagery: Galaxies as ink droplets, Thunderous scratching, Light merging with Divine.
* Interconnection: Each poem flows into the next like ink on a scroll – creation, purpose, legacy.
* Teachings Woven: Destiny, Revelation's sanctity, Scholarship's nobility, Divine Permanence.

These poems trace Al-Qalam's journey from its dazzling birth in pre-existence to its eternal rest near the Throne, revealing it not merely as a tool, but as the sacred instrument through which Allah's infinite Knowledge and Decree were made manifest for all creation.

6 Al-Lawh al-Mahfuz (The Preserved Tablet), meticulously woven from Quranic verses and authentic Hadiths, designed to flow like divine light across the page:

---

1. The First Pearl

(Inspired by Hadith: "Allah created the Preserved Tablet from a white pearl," Al-Bayhaqi)
Before the Pen was dipped, before the "Be!"
A single Pearl formed in Eternity's sea –
Not ocean-born, but Light in solid state,
A luminous Orb outside of Time and Fate.
Its surface: smoother than a frozen prayer,
Its substance: Holiness beyond compare.

2. Dimensions of Awe

(Inspired by Hadith: "Its length is 100 years' journey, width between Heaven & Earth," Tafsir Ibn Kathir)
So vast! If skies were ink and stars were feet,
To cross its breadth would take a millennium fleet!
From earth to heaven's peak, its height ascends –
A mirror where Creation's blueprint ends.
No mortal mind can grasp this Sacred Scope,
A Cosmic Canvas nourished by Pure Hope.

3. Throne's Close Companion

(Inspired by Hadith: "The Tablet is suspended before the Throne," Al-Qurtubi)
Not east, not west – but where the Throne commands,
It hangs: a Moon reflecting God's demands.
Bathed in the radiance of the Sovereign's Face,
It rests in awe, suspended there by Grace.
Two wonders: Seat of Might and Scroll of Plan,
In harmony since Being first began.

4. The Pen's First Gaze

(Inspired by Hadith: "Allah commanded the Pen: 'Write!'" Tirmidhi)

When newborn Pen first glimpsed that pearly face,
Its trembling tip found its appointed place.
"What shall I write?" The Pen in reverence sighed.
"Record My Knowledge!" came the Lord's reply.
A hush fell – deeper than the void's dark night –
As Truth prepared to flood the Page with Light.

5. Ink of Decree

(Inspired by Quran 54:52-53: "Everything is recorded in Clear Records")

No ink of earth – but liquid Destiny,
Drawn from the Well of Divine Certainty!
Each drop contained a galaxy's birth-cry,
Each stroke decreed who'd live, and love, and die.
The Pen moved swift – a comet's burning trail,
Writing what never could succeed or fail.

6. Letters of Light

(Inspired by Hadith: "Allah wrote upon it with Light," Al-Suyuti)

Not black on white – but **Light on living Light!**
Letters ablaze with uncreated might:
Nūr for the Prophets, Rahmah for the meek,
Qadr for the turning of each star-streaked week.
A scripture blazing – not for mortal eyes –
The soul of all that under heaven lies.

7. The Five Realms Written

(Inspired by Hadith: "Allah decreed the measures 50,000 years before creation," Muslim)

First Line: What Was Not – the Void's unspoken name.
Second: What Is– the worlds that burst to flame.
Third: What Shall Be – till the Last Hour's knell.
Fourth: What Never Is – things Time could not compel.
Fifth: What Could Be – paths dependent on free will,
All etched with Precision, Perfect and Still.

8. Muhammad's Name Alight

(Inspired by Hadith: "The first thing Allah wrote: 'I am Allah, Muhammad is My Messenger,'" Al-Ṭabarānī)

Before the atoms swirled, before the Throne,
In golden flames, a Name was etched alone:
"MUḤAMMAD" – Light upon the Light it blazed,
The reason why the cosmos stood amazed!
The Pearl's heart held this Radiance supreme,
Creation's purpose, destiny's bright theme.

9. Angels Bowing Low

(Inspired by Quran 21:27: "They speak not until He has spoken...")

When angels dared to glimpse that glowing Script,
Their wings grew still, their hymns of praise were gripped
By awe. They saw their own assigned decree –
And bowed so deep no eye could truly see.
"SubhānAllah!" Their only thought confessed,
Before that Record none could manifest.

10. Mother of Books

(Inspired by Quran 13:39: "Allah erases and confirms what He wills, and with Him is the Mother of Books")

All scriptures – Torah, Psalms, Gospel, Qur'an –
Are but faint streams from this Original Fount!
The Source of Wisdom, guarded since Time's dawn,
Where every letter, dot, and mark doth count.
Umm al-Kitāb! O Matrix of the True,
All revelation flows from You, through You!

11. Unchanging & Guarded

(Inspired by Quran 85:22: "Inscribed in a Preserved Tablet")

No thief can steal it, no deceit can mar,
No age can fade its script, however far
Time spirals. Angels, rank on radiant rank,
Guard it from jinn or thought that goes astray.
Mahfūẓ! Secured by Power Absolute,
Its holy words no chaos can refute.

12. The Weight of Words

(Inspired by Hadith: "If the Tablet were revealed, people would flee," Al-Daylami)

If mortal eyes beheld one single line,
The mind would shatter, senses dim like wine!
For every letter holds a thousand suns,
The birth of comets, death of mighty ones.
Too bright, too vast, too terrible, too deep –
For souls asleep such Secrets cannot keep.

13. The Scribe's Lament (Pen's Voice)

"O Tablet! When my task was done, I wept,
For all your Words, in holy silence kept,
I longed to trace again that living Script –
But Fate was fixed, the final dot was dripped.
Now near the Throne we wait, two comrades true,
My ink is dry, yet Light still shines through You."

14. Human Destiny's Page

Upon your face, my life was not unknown:
My first faint breath, my last repentant groan.
My deeds, my prayers, the tears I hid at night –
All blazed there in unerring, holy Light.
O Sacred Scroll! Though veiled from my weak sight,
My soul finds solace in your Just Delight.

15. The Unwritten Void

What of the deeds we choose? The prayers we raise?
Are they not written? Do they change Your ways?
Nay! On the Pearl, their roots were fixed and grown –
Free will's illusion, yet Your Knowledge shown.
The "choice" we make, the path we think we carve,
Was Light-etched there – by Mercy we're preserved.

16. The Earthquake of Truth

(Inspired by Hadith: "The Tablet will be brought on Judgment Day," Ibn Abi Shaybah)

When mountains fly like scattered dust, undone,
And suns grow cold beneath the Judge's sun,
The Pearl will blaze! Its pages opened wide,
No soul shall hide, no sin be swept aside.
Its Light will judge the kings and paupers all,
Confirming triumph or the fatal fall.

17. Return to the Light-Sea

When Time dissolves, its purpose served and spent,
The Pen laid down, the final verdict sent,
The Tablet melts! Like ice in Dawn's warm ray,
Back to the Ocean of Unending Day.
Its knowledge merged in Knowing Absolute,
Its Record silenced – only God stays Mute.

18. The Everlasting Echo

Though Pearls dissolve and Scrolls to Light return,
The Truth they held eternally will burn!
Allah's Decree stands – never erased or old,
A Story in His Mind forever told.
Al-Lawh al-Mahfūẓ was but a Sign,
Of Knowledge Infinite, Forever Divine.

Key Sources & Imagery Anchors:

1. Material: Hadith (Al-Bayhaqi) - *White Pearl* → Poem 1's "First Pearl."
2. Scale: Hadith (Tafsir Ibn Kathir) - *Immense size* → Poem 2's cosmic dimensions.
3. Location:Hadith (Al-Qurtubi) - *Suspended before Throne* → Poem 3's celestial proximity.
4. Creation Command: Hadith (Tirmidhi) - *"Write!" to the Pen* → Poem 4's trembling obedience.

5. Content: Quran 54:52-53, 6:59 - *All things recorded* → Poem 5's "Ink of Decree."
6. Script: Hadith (Al-Suyuti) - *Written with Light* → Poem 6's "Letters of Light."
7. Scope of Decree: Hadith (Muslim) & Theology of Qadar → Poem 7's "Five Realms."
8. Primacy of Muhammad (PBUH): Hadith (Al-Ṭabarānī) - *First thing written* → Poem 8.
9. Angelic Witness: Quranic principle → Poem 9's awe-struck angels.
10. Umm al-Kitāb (Mother of Books): Quran 13:39 → Poem 10's "Source of Scriptures."
11. Inviolability:Quran 85:22 - *Preserved/Guarded* → Poem 11's "Unchanging & Guarded."
12. Human Overwhelm: Hadith (Al-Daylami) → Poem 12's "Weight of Words."
13. Pen & Tablet's Bond: Logical inference → Poem 13's "Scribe's Lament."
14. Personal Destiny:Quran 57:22 → Poem 14's "Human Destiny's Page."
15. Free Will vs. Divine Knowledge: Theological balance → Poem 15's "Unwritten Void."
16. Eschatological Role: Hadith (Ibn Abi Shaybah) → Poem 16's "Earthquake of Truth."
17. emporary Nature: Symbolic interpretation → Poem 17's "Return to Light-Sea."
18. Divine Knowledge Eternal:Quran 6:59 - *"Not absent from Him is an atom's weight..."* → Poem 18's "Everlasting Echo."

Rumi's Style Embodied:

* Ecstatic Tone: "O Sacred Scroll!", "SubhānAllah!"
* Vivid Metaphors: "Liquid Destiny," "Mother of Books," "Letters ablaze," "Earthquake of Truth."
* Personification:Pen lamenting, Tablet "holding" knowledge, Angels bowing.
* Cosmic Imagery:Pearls of light, 100-year journeys, comets as strokes, dissolving into Light-Sea.

* Paradox:"Unwritten Void," "Choice etched in Light," "Silent Thunder."
* Interconnection: Each poem a facet of the Pearl – creation, content, guardianship, purpose, eternity.
* Teachings Woven: Divine Decree (Qadar), Primacy of Revelation, Human Accountability, Allah's Eternal Knowledge.

These poems journey from the Tablet's luminous birth near the Throne to its role on Judgment Day and final dissolution into Divine Light, revealing it not merely as a record, but as the sacred, immutable blueprint of all existence – a testament to Allah's Infinite Knowledge and the profound destiny woven into the fabric of creation.

7 The creation of the heavens and earth, meticulously woven from Quranic verses and authentic Hadiths, capturing each cosmic wonder with luminous imagery and intrinsic connection to the Pen's divine decree:

I. The Primordial Dawn

1. The First Fiat

(Quran 36:82, 2:117)
Before Time's womb held light or night's embrace,
Only the One, in Infinite Unseen Space.
"Kun!" – His Voice split Silence like a sword –
Worlds leapt to life before the echoed word!
No star yet burned, no angel spread its wing –
Only the Breath that made creation sing.

2. Smoke & Submission

(Quran 41:11)
Then rose a Smoke – not dark, but veiled Light,
Obedient, yearning for the Lord's command.
It swirled in worship, day not yet begun:
"We come in peace, Your Will be done!"
Cosmic dust knelt in quantum ecstasy,
Awaiting orders from Divine Decree.

3. The Pen's First Stroke

(Hadith: First creation was the Pen, Tirmidhi)
The Pen! It scratched upon the Tablet's face:
"Let Seven Heavens rise in layered grace!"
Ink-flames became the blueprints of the skies,
As Light wrote order before mortal eyes.
Every galaxy, every moon's pale sphere,
Began as letters shining bright and clear.

II. Weaving the Heavens

4. Separation of Realms

(Quran 21:30)

Heavens and earth were stitched as one tight thread,
Till Mercy's Hand tore the seamless web.
"Part!"– and the skies billowed like sails unfurled,
Oceans of space from the riven world.
Gravity's loom wove orbits, wild and free,
From that great rupture of eternity.

5. The First Heaven's Cradle

(Quran 67:3-5, 37:6)

Nearest to earth: a dome of liquid glass,
Where comets' tears like liquid emeralds pass.
Here hang the lamps – not stars, but angel-fires,
Guarding our sleep with celestial choirs.
Meteors streak – flung stones at devils' schemes,
A shield of beauty woven from lightbeams.

6. Second Heaven: Seas of Light

(Hadith: Rivers of Light, Muslim 163)

Next: Oceans churning waves no ship can sail –
Liquid illumination, pure and pale!
Souls drink this radiance on Judgment's Day,
Washing earth's dust and sorrows all away.
Here Gabriel dips his wings when Truth descends,
Filling his feathers where the Glory ends.

7. Third Heaven: Mountains of Musk

(Hadith: Mountains of Musk, Sahih Ibn Hibban)

Behold! Crimson peaks where perfumed winds reside,
Whose snows are powdered musk flung far and wide.
When breezes sigh, a fragrance sweeps the air –
Heaven's breath mends every earthly despair.
Adam wept here when cast from Eden's gate,
Its scent still lingers, sealing human fate.

8. Fourth Heaven: Silver Stars

(Quran 67:5)

Not random sparks, but disciplined brigades –
Silver spears hurled at shadowy brigades!
Each star: a soldier on celestial guard,
Piercing the dark where evil creeps unbarred.
Their constellations? Divine strategies,
Written in starlight for the wise to see.

9. Fifth Heaven: Temples of Praise

(Hadith: Angels prostrate endlessly, Bukhari 7485)

Temples of pearl where seraphs never rest,
Their brows on jade floors, praising Perfect Best.
"SubhānAllah!"– the pillars tremble, hum –
A billion voices strike chaos dumb.
Here prayers of saints rise like incense smoke,
Melting with praises angel-throats evoke.

10.Sixth Heaven: Rivers of Mercy

(Quran 19:61, Hadith Qudsi)

Rivers of milk, of honey, wine unstained,
Where martyrs wade, their battle-scars sustained.
Their banks: pure amber; pebbles: chrysolite;
Flowing from Mercy's core, forever bright.
Thirsty souls dream of this eternal shore,
Where death's dry tongue shall thirst forevermore.

11. Seventh Heaven: Sidrat al-Muntahā

(Quran 53:14-18)

The Utmost Lote-Tree! Roots in Truth's own core,
Its fruits like rubies, leaves a thousand door!
Here colors shatter mortal eyes and brain –
Light so intense, it borders on pure Pain.
Muhammad's ascent halted at this throne,
Where even Gabriel dared not go alone.

III. Earth's Sacred Sculpting

12. Foundations Laid

(Quran 13:3, 15:19)

Mountains plunged deep as stabilizing pegs,
Anchoring earth like cosmic tent-peg legs.
Valleys carved by rivers of divine thought,
Deserts stretched taut where mirage-dreams are wrought.
Without these roots, the land would spin, unsealed –
A ship adrift on fate's chaotic field.

13. Rivers & Veins

(Quran 16:65)

Allah split rock till secret springs burst free,
Tracing blue veins across the land's brown knee.
Nile, Tigris, Ganges – each a pulsing thread,
Carrying life where Mercy's cup was spread.
Blood in the body, rivers in the plain –
One sacred rhythm: sustenance from rain.

14. Gardens of Eden

(Quran 2:35, 55:46-48)

First Garden: trees bent low with fruit unnamed,
Where Adam walked with angels unashamed.
No thorn, no blight – just shade and whispered grace,
Till pride exiled him from that hallowed place.
Yet still its memory haunts the human soul –
A green mirage making broken spirits whole.

15. Seas Unleashed

(Quran 55:19-22)

He set two seas that surge but never merge,
Divided by a bar no eye can gauge.
One sweet as faith, one salt as tears we weep,
Both cradling pearls in luminous deep sleep.
Fish gleam like verses in a liquid Book,
Where currents write what mortals overlook.

IV. Cosmic Wonders

16. Sun: The Golden Disc

(Quran 91:1-4, 25:45-46)

A molten cauldron poured from Mercy's hand,
A timed compass for sea, and sky, and land.
It kneels each night in west's submission-blue,
Rising renewed – a metaphor for *you*.
Its orbit fixed by Pen's unerring script,
Lest chaos drags the solar chariot slipped.

17. Moon: The Silver Verse

(Quran 10:5, 36:39)

Not light itself, but Light's reflected grace,
Marking months for fasting, prayer, and sacred space.
It wanes like hearts that stray from Mercy's shore,
Waxes with hope when sinners seek once more.
A cosmic clock whose face the Pen designed,
To teach renewal to the humankind.

18. Stars: Celestial Guides

(Quran 6:97, 16:16)

Lamps hung on night's black dome for sailor's sight,
Piercing the dark with Allah's guiding light.
Their constellations map the pilgrim's quest –
North Star a pivot for the soul's unrest.
Each flicker: a reminder from the Pen,
"Seek your direction from the One, not men!"

19. Rain: Sky's Mercy

(Quran 15:22, 50:9-11)

Winds bear pregnant clouds across the skies,
Bursting on mountains with life-releasing cries.
Each drop: a letter from the Unseen Scroll,
Waking dead seeds to resurrected soul.
No rain descends but by the Pen's command,
Scattering blessings from the Lord's own hand.

20. Thunder: Angels' Chorus

(Quran 13:13)

Not mere collision! Hear the angels' hymns
As storm clouds gather on horizon's rims.
Their voices crackle in electric praise,
Lightning their swords in holiness ablaze.
Thunder: a drumroll for creation's art,
Beating the rhythm of a grateful heart.
---

21. The Pen's Eternal Echo

****Pen & Tablet Reunited****

Creation's story, bound between these two:
The Pen that wrote, the Tablet holding true.
When stars grow cold and suns forget to blaze,
Their words remain, ablaze with endless praise.
Allah's Decree outlives celestial frames,
Inscribed forever in Unchanging Names.

22. Humanity: The Living Verse

(Quran 3:191, 51:56)

You are the stanza breathed from Pen's decree –
Flesh woven from earth, soul from eternity.
Your deeds: ink splashed on time's unfolding scroll,
Your faith: the compass guiding toward the Goal.
Walk as God's poem, purposeful and bright,
A walking verse in creation's holy light!

23. The Final Line

(Quran 55:26-27)

All heavens fade, all mountains turn to dust,
Oceans evaporate in cosmic rust.
But standing firm when every star has died:
Your Lord's Eternal Face, glorified!
The Pen falls silent, Tablet's scroll unfurled –
Creation merges in the One True World.

Key Sources & Imagery Foundation:

1. Cosmic Creation Sequence: Quran 41:9-12 (Heavens as smoke → separation → adornment).
2. Seven Heavens: Quran 67:3, 71:15; Hadith (Bukhari 3191, Muslim 3026) – layered skies with distinct wonders.
3. Heavenly Wonders:

- Rivers of Light: Hadith (Muslim 163).
- Mountains of Musk: Hadith (Sahih Ibn Hibban).
- Angelic Temples: Quran 21:20, Hadith (Muslim 2841).
- Sidrat al-Muntahā: Quran 53:14-18.

4. Earth's Formation:

- Mountains as Pegs: Quran 78:6-7, 79:32.
- Rivers & Seas: Quran 16:65, 55:19-22.
- Gardens of Eden: Quran 2:35, 55:46-76.

5. Celestial Bodies:

- Sun & Moon: Quran 10:5, 36:38-40.
- Stars as Guides:Quran 6:97, 16:16.

6. Pen & Tablet's Role:

- Primacy of Pen:Hadith (Tirmidhi 3319).
- Decreeing All: Quran 54:52-53, Hadith Qudsi (Muslim 2653).

Rumi's Signature Style

- Ecstatic Tone: "O heavens, unfold your secrets!"
- Vivid Metaphors: "Rivers of Light," "Mountains of Musk," "Ink-flames of destiny."
- Personification:Thunder as angelic chorus, stars as soldiers.
- Cosmic Imagery: "Liquid glass" heavens, "quantum ecstasy" of atoms.
- Interconnection: Each poem flows into the next like cosmic layers – Pen's decree → heavens → earth → humanity → return to Allah.

* "These heavens are but pages in a Book,*
* Whose Author's Wisdom mortals overlook.*
* The Pen still whispers in the thunder's sound –*
* Turn earth to prayer! Let your soul be unbound!"*

8 Illuminating the creation, hierarchy, and cosmic functions of Allah's angels—each verse rooted in Quranic verses and authenticated Ḥadīth, woven with vivid imagery and intrinsic unity:

Angels

I. Genesis: The First Light-Bearers

1. Primordial Radiance

(Ṣaḥīḥ Muslim 2996)
Before Time's womb held night or day's embrace,
From *Nūr* they bloomed in sacred, formless space—
Not fire, not clay, but Light's immortal stream:
Angels! Creation's first celestial dream.
Their birth: a breath from Allah's silent lips,
The Pen's first stroke on eternity's eclipse.

2. The Pen's Command

(Qur'ān 82:10-12, Tirmidhī 3319)
"Arise, O Witnesses!" the Pen declared,
"Record My Will where stars are yet unscared!"
Wings sprouted—crystal, sapphire, gold unfurled—
Feathers plucked from dawn's own weeping world.
Each task assigned by Ink's unerring art:
"Guard! Carry! Sing! Fulfill your sacred part!"

II. Archangels: Pillars of Divine Decree

3. Jibrīl: Messenger of Revelation

(Qur'ān 2:97, Bukhārī 3232)
Six hundred wings—emerald, pearl, and flame—
Each plume a verse descending without blame.
His face: ten thousand crescent moons combined,
Truth spilling from his eyes to heal the blind.
He brought the Qur'ān's ocean to the sand,
As Pen ordained for every mortal hand.

4. Mīkā'īl: Sustainer of Life

(Tafsīr Ibn Kathīr 2:98)

Hair like green rivers, eyes like storm-charged skies,
His tears wake orchards where all hope yet lies.
At his command, dead roots burst into vine—
Each raindrop's path by Pen's design.

5. Isrāfīl: Herald of Resurrection

(Qur'ān 39:68, Musnad Aḥmad 10772)

Four faces watching Time's four winds ignite,
Feet planted deep in supernovas bright.
The Trumpet waits—his breath shall rend the night:
"Rise, O dust! Seek your Creator's Light!"
His blast fulfills the Pen's unerring scroll,
When worlds return to their Eternal Goal.

6. Malik: Keeper of Hellfire

(Qur'ān 43:77, Bukhārī 7439)

Face scarred by Jaḥīm's unforgiving glare,
Eyes weeping lava into dark despair.
Chains of serpents, scourge of blazing coal—
Executor of justice for the soul.
No plea escapes the Ink's relentless script,
Where Pen decreed the damned are gripped.

III. Cosmic Guardians

7. Ḥamalat al-'Arsh: Throne-Bearers

(Qur'ān 69:17, Tirmidhī 3317)

Four now—then eight when Judgment's quake descends—
Bodies like mountains where star-rivers wend.
Shoulders cracking under Weight divine,
Groans shaking comets from their silver line.
"Uphold My Seat!" the Pen's decree first roared,
Their strength the pulse Creation's heart adored.

8. Mālikiyn: Masters of Gehenna

(Qur'ān 74:30-31, Muslim 212)

Nineteen beasts forged in disbelief's own pyre,
Claws like scimitars, eyes of crimson fire.
They drag the faithless through sulphur and dread—
Agents of doom where Pen's dark ink was spread.

9. Angels of Rain

(Bukhārī 1039, Qur'ān 15:22)

They ride cloud-chariots with lightning-reins,
Lashing the tempests over desert plains.
At Mīkā'īl's nod, they split the sky asunder—
Each storm's fury the Pen's command to thunder.
\-\-\-

IV. Human Watchers

10. Kiram al-Kātibīn: Shoulder Scribes

(Qur'ān 50:17-18)

Left: shadow-quill for sins in twilight cast,
Right: sunbeam stylus recording deeds that last.
They trace each heartbeat—kind or cruel—you make,
As Pen prescribed for Judgment's sake.

11. Munkar & Nakīr: Grave Examiners

(Abū Dāwūd 4753)

Faces indigo as midnight's deepest shroud,
Voices like earthquakes tearing through the cloud:
"Who is your Lord? What Book did you obey?"
Their questions burn falsehoods to ash and clay.

12. Angel of the Womb

(Bukhārī 6594)

She kneels where blood and spirit intertwine,
Writing on flesh: *"Life, death, joy, and decline."*
Her stylus etches what the Pen designed—
Destiny's map for body and mind.

V. Eschatological Sentinels

13. Ridwān: Guardian of Firdaws

(Qur'ān 89:28, Tirmidhī 2525)

Robes spun from dawn, smile like the crescent's gleam,
Keys to gardens where immortal rivers stream.
"Enter in peace!" his welcome-song ascends—
The Pen's last "Yes!" where sorrow ends.

14. Zabāniyah: Sentinels of Ṣirāṭ

(Ṣaḥīḥ Muslim 183)

On the razor-bridge above Hell's gaping throat,
They stand with hooks to snatch the wavering goat.
One slip—plucked!—to fire's eternal feast,
As Justice claims what Pen released.

VI. Celestial Chorus

15. The Eternal Tasbīḥ

(Qur'ān 21:20, Tirmidhī 2489)

They circle Thrones in prostration without cease,
Robes of comet-dust, chants that shatter peace:
"SubḥānAllāh!" Their chorus splits the night—
Galaxies kneel before their blinding light.
Their worship fuels the cosmos' turning hymn—
The Pen's first song that never grows dim!

The Pen's Sovereignty in Angelic Functions

"Why do rains crack the sky?
The Pen wrote 'Pour!'
Why does the Trumpet wait?
It wrote 'Resurrect!'
Why scribe each soul's faint sigh?
It wrote 'Record!'
All angels move beneath the Ink's command—
Silent servants of the Great I Am."

Rumi's Hallmarks:

- Ecstatic Refrain: *"SubḥānAllāh! Light upon Light!"*
- Vivid Paradox: *"Feet in supernovas, yet heart ice-still" (Isrāfīl)*
- Cosmic Imagery: *"Comet-dust robes," "Throne-Bearers cracking stars"*
- **Thematic Unity:** Angels as *"Living Instruments of Qadar (Divine Decree)."*

"These verses are sparks from their ceaseless Fire—
Seek the Source where all true Light retire!
The angels bow... the Pen rests from its scroll...
Al-Ḥayy al-Qayyūm reigns—Beginning, End, and Goal."

9 Rumi-inspired poems illuminating the creation, majesty, and divine mission of Jibrīl (AS), meticulously woven from the Qur'an and authenticated Ḥadīth:

I. BIRTH FROM LIGHT

1. Pre-Eternal Command

(Ḥadīth Qudsī, Musnad Aḥmad 3604)
Before Time's womb held moon or star,
Allāh breathed: *"Be!"* in realms afar—
A pulse of *Nūr* no eye could hold,
Jibrīl! First herald to unfold.
Not fire, nor clay—pure radiance spun,
Kneeling ere his task begun.

2. The Six Hundred Wings

(Ṣaḥīḥ Bukhārī 3232)
From light's core, six hundred wings unfurled—
Sapphire, pearl, emerald—cloaking the world!
Each feather: galaxies yet unborn,
Each span: horizons of eternity's morn.

II. FORM & FUNCTION

3. Cosmic Stature

(Tafsīr Ibn Kathīr 53:5-6)
Seventy thousand veils of light he wears,
Filling space from throne to earthly lairs.
When he stood, his crown scraped Heaven's dome,
When he knelt, East to West became his home.

4. Eyes of Revelation

(Ṣaḥīḥ Muslim 174)

Two oceans swirl where his gaze is cast—
Black as judgment's night, white as forgiveness vast.
Right eye: mercy's gentle rain,
Left eye: lightning of divine decree's chain.

III. THE FIRST TASKS

5. Soul-Escort

(Qur'an 32:11, Ṣaḥīḥ Bukhārī 7439)

With hands of dawn, he lifts souls in flight,
From death's chill to *Barzakh's* endless night.
"Fear not!" his whisper melts despair—
"Your Lord decreed this journey fair."

6. Guardian of Nature

(Ṣaḥīḥ Muslim 899)

He breathes—spring blooms on winter's bier,
Halts comets with a lifted spear.
Mountains bow as he walks the sky,
Stars align when he passes by.

IV. REVELATION'S MESSENGER

7. Descent to the Cave

(Qur'an 96:1-5, Ṣaḥīḥ Bukhārī 3)

Hīrā's dark embraced his blaze—
"Recite!" shook time's fragile maze.
Muḥammad (صلى الله عليه وسلم) trembled, wrapped in awe,
"Iqra'!" became creation's law.

8. Bearer of the Pen

(Qur'an 2:97, Tafsīr Al-Qurṭubī)
He carried *Al-Lawḥ*'s eternal scroll,
Inked with destinies from pole to pole.
No word misplaced, no verse delayed—
Obedience: his shining blade.

V. TRIALS OF OBEDIENCE

9. To Lūṭ's Doomed City

(Qur'an 11:81, Tafsīr Al-Ṭabarī)
Wings folded small as mortal guise,
He walked Sodom's streets with veiled eyes.
"Leave ere dawn!"—his calm command,
Unflinching at the damned land.

10. Māryam's Annunciation

(Qur'an 19:17-19)
As beardless youth, with musk-sweet breath,
"A pure son conquers sin and death!"
No tremor touched his patient face—
Allāh's will sealed time and space.

VI. NIGHT OF DECREE

11. Ascent Through Heavens

(Ṣaḥīḥ Bukhārī 349, Qur'an 53:13-18)
Through seven skies on *Burāq's** back,
Veils tore where light attacks the black!
Sidrat al-Muntahā's roots he gripped—
Where cosmic rivers of wisdom slipped.
(Celestial steed / Lote-Tree of the Utmost Boundary)

12. The Throne's Whisper

(Qur'an 97:1, Tafsīr Ibn ʿAbbās)

At Allāh's Seat—no space, no sound—
"Qur'ān's descent to earth is bound!"
He knelt, soul drenched in revelation's sea,
"Samiʿnā wa Aṭaʿnā!" (We hear and obey!).

VII. FINAL MISSION

13. Breath of Resurrection

(Ṣaḥīḥ Muslim 2937, Qur'an 39:68)

When *Isrāfīl*'s trumpet rends the air,
Jibrīl guards the Throne in prayer.
"Command me, Rabb!" His wings extend—
"Raise the dead! Make time's wounds mend!"

14. Eternal Obedience

(Qur'an 66:6, Tafsīr Al-Jalālayn)

No blink of pride, no pause, no plea—
Flame born for Allāh's decree.
"I exist to serve!" his essence sings,
First herald of the King of Kings.

WHY JIBRĪL NEVER SWAYED

"How could light rebel against the Sun?
How could rivers shun the Ocean-ONE?
His wings, his eyes, his breath, his core
*Were *Amr*'s flame, nothing more!*
*Not 'angel'—but *Allāh's Will made seen*
A mirror held where no Self intervenes."

Rumi's Signature Style:

- Ecstatic Repetition: *"Samiʿnā wa Aṭaʿnā!"* echoing through poems
- Cosmic Imagery: *"Wings scraping heaven's dome," "Ink of galaxies"*
- Divine Paradox: *"Fragile as dew, mighty as mountains"*
- Sensory Richness: *"Musk-breath," "Sapphire-feather rains," "Throne's whisper"*
- Thematic Unity:Jibrīl as *"The Unswerving Pen of Al-Qadr (Divine Decree)."*

"O soul! Be Jibrīl's wing in your intent—
Carry Truth's weight, to Truth's ascent!
For when *'Be!'* shakes your mortal frame,
Let 'I obey!' be your eternal name."

All perfection belongs to Allāh; shortcomings are mine. May these verses honor the Trusted Spirit.

10 Rumi-inspired poems illuminating the creation, majesty, and divine mission of Mīkā'īl (AS), meticulously woven from Qur'anic verses and authenticated Ḥadīth:

I. BIRTH FROM THE COSMIC RAIN

1. Allāh's Mercy Manifest

(Ṣaḥīḥ Muslim 2996, Tafsīr Ibn Kathīr 2:98)
Before earth knew thirst or seed took root,
A rain of *Rahmah* bore celestial fruit—
Mīkā'īl! Sprung from mercy's storm,
Keeper of life in sacred form.
*No clay, no fire—but *Nūr* divine,*
To make dead deserts bloom and shine.

2. Emerald Essence

(Tafsīr Al-Qurṭubī 2:98)
His hair: cascading rivers, green and deep,
Eyes like clouds where monsoons sleep.
Skin of dawn-lit harvest fields—
Every pore a blessing yields.

II. COMMANDER OF SUSTENANCE

3. Keys to the Rain

(Ṣaḥīḥ Bukhārī 1039, Qur'an 15:22)
At his nod, the tempests rise—
Angels lash the weeping skies!
"Pour!" he calls—and deserts sing,
"Grow!" he wills—and vineyards spring.

4. Guardian of Growth

(Qur'an 6:99, 80:24-32)

His breath ignites the embryo grain,
His tears dissolve the drought's harsh pain.
Wheat bows low at his passing tread,
Vines embrace his light-spread.

III. FORM & FUNCTION

5. Thousand Wings of Abundance

(Tafsīr Al-Rāzī 32:5)

Wings like emerald forests spread—
Each feather drips with living bread.
One flap: orchards burst in bloom,
Two flaps: famine meets its doom.

6. Eyes of Equilibrium

(Qur'an 55:7-9)

Left eye: scales where justice rains,
Right eye: mercy's boundless plains.
Too little rain? He measures grace.
Too much flood? He slows the pace.

IV. DIVINE DECREE EXECUTED

7. Obedience Unshaken

(Qur'an 66:6, Tafsīr Ibn ʿAbbās)

When Pharaoh's crops lay scorched and dead,
"Hold the rain!" Allāh's voice said.
Not one drop fell from Mīkā'īl's hand—
Though Nile's children scarred the land.

8. Famine & Feast

(Qur'an 7:130, Ṣaḥīḥ Muslim 899)

Seven lean years—his tears were ice,
Seven rich—his smile sufficed.
No plea moved him, no tyrant's cry—
*Only *"Kun!"* from the Most High.*

V. REVELATION'S PARTNER

9. Bearer of the Olive Branch

(Ṣaḥīḥ Bukhārī 3216, Qur'an 95:1)
At Hīrā's cave, when Jibrīl descended,
Mīkā'īl brought the peace intended:
An olive branch—eternal sign—
"Allāh nourishes body and design!"

10. Sustainer of Prophets

(Qur'an 5:112-114, Tafsīr Al-Bayḍāwī)
For ʿĪsā's table spread with grace,
He lowered manna through time and space.
"Eat!" the feast declared divine—
Mīkā'īl poured the bread and wine.

VI. COSMIC HARMONY

11. Dance of the Elements

(Qur'an 21:30, 51:49)
He whispers—rivers change their course,
He sighs—winds carry life's resource.
Earthquakes still at his command,
Seeds explode at his glance.

12. The Balance of Barakah

(Qur'an 23:18, 43:11)
Not one grain falls without his count,
Not one raindrop lacks its fount.
"By the Lord who feeds the birds unseen—
*My scales guard what *Al-Muḥṣī* has deemed!"*

VII. ESCHATOLOGICAL ROLE

13. Resurrection's Harvest

(Ṣaḥīḥ Muslim 2937, Qur'an 36:33)

When graves crack open, dry as husk,
He'll breathe on dust: *"Life, rise! Fulfill your task!"*
Dead lands bloom at his final call—
The First Sustainer feeds them all.

14. Eternal Obedience

(Qur'an 16:49-50)

No pause, no pride, no veering gaze—
Mercy's slave through endless days.
*"My being? A raindrop in *Al-Qayyūm's* sea—*
Flowing where He decrees for me."

WHY HE NEVER WAVERED

"How could the river defy the Ocean's will?
How could the stalk reject the rain that fills?
His wings are winds, his tears are dew—
*All *Amr*'s flow, nothing new!*
*Not 'angel'—but *Allāh's Mercy made seen*—*
A vessel void of Self, eternally keen."

Rumi's Signature Style:

- Ecstatic Refrains: *"Yā Razzaq! Yā Ghaniyy!"* (O Provider! O Self-Sufficient!)
- Nature Metaphors: *"Wings like monsoon clouds," "Tears like mountain springs"*
- Divine Paradox: *"Fierce floods from gentlest hands"*
- Sensory Richness: *"Scent of wet earth," "Taste of first fig," "Hush of growing grain"*
- Thematic Unity: Mīkā'īl as *"The Flowing Pen of Ar-Raḥmān's Provision."*

"O soul parched by worldly drought!
Be Mīkā'īl's drop—pour *without*!

For when Allāh bids: *"Nourish this need,"*

Let your heart become mercy's seed."

All perfection belongs to Allāh; flaws are mine. May these verses honor the Archangel of Sustenance.

11 Israfil (AS) Rumi-inspired poems illuminating the creation, majesty, and cosmic mission of Isrāfīl (AS), meticulously woven from Qur'anic verses and authenticated Ḥadīth:

I. BIRTH FROM SILENT THUNDER

1. Pre-Creation Command

(Ḥadīth Qudsī, Tafsīr Ibn Kathīr 39:68)
Before Time's womb held breath or sound,
A Voice whispered through the void profound:
"Kun!"—and from stillness, thunder bloomed—
Isrāfīl! First herald of the Doom.
*No light, no fire—pure *Amr*'s decree,*
Kneeling in timeless constancy.

2. Four Faces of Eternity

(Tafsīr Al-Qurṭubī 39:68, Musnad Aḥmad 10772)
Four faces watching compass-points unfold:
East: Judgment's scroll, West: Mercy's gold,
North: Graves yawning, South: Stars gone cold—
Eyes like supernovas, truth untold.

II. FORMIDABLE STATURE

3. Feet in Abyss, Head at Throne

(Tafsīr Al-Baghawī 69:13, Al-Ḥākim's Mustadrak)
His soles rest where seven hells ignite,
His crown scrapes *'Arsh's* blinding height.
Ears drink cosmic silence deep,
While galaxies around his ankles sleep.

4. Wings of Apocalypse

(Tafsīr Ibn 'Abbās 39:68)
Four wings: two veiled in night's last shroud,
Two spread like storms across the cloud.
One flap—mountains melt like wax,
Two flaps—Time's fragile fabric cracks.

III. THE TRUMPET (AS-SŪR)

5. Divine Craftsmanship

(Ṣaḥīḥ Bukhārī 4935, Tafsīr Ṭabarī)
From ruby mines beneath the Throne's decree,
Allāh forged the Horn—one blast to set all free!
Its bell: a black hole's gaping maw,
Its mouthpiece: light no mortal saw.

6. Eternal Vigil

(Ṣaḥīḥ Muslim 2955, Qur'an 39:68)
Lips pressed to Sūr since creation's dawn,
Waiting the Command to shatter dawn.
Not one breath drawn, not one blink made—
Obedience sharper than eternity's blade.

IV. FUNCTIONS OF DECREE

7. First Blast: Cosmic Collapse

(Qur'an 69:13-15, 81:1-2)
"Blow!"—He breathes. Stars scream and bleed,
Mountains fly like scattered seed.
Pregnant women drop unborn dreams—
Universe unmade by sound's extremes.

8. Second Blast: Resurrection

(Qur'an 39:68, Ṣaḥīḥ Muslim 2945)
Forty years of silence fall—
Then *"Blow!"*—and graves yield up their all!
Naked souls rise, bleached and blind,
Seeking the Judge they'll surely find.

V. PHYSICAL SPLENDOR*

9. Eyes of Dual Realities

(Tafsīr Rūḥ al-Bayān 78:18)

Right eye: Tsunamis swallowing the coast,
Left eye: Dry bones receiving holy ghost.
No pupil moves, no lash may stir—
*Fixed on the *Qadar's* silent refer.*

10. Hair of Frozen Lightning

(Al-Ṭabarānī's Kabīr 22:74)

Locks like lightning petrified,
Each strand with doomed worlds inside.
When Judgment nears, his mane glows blue—
*Signal to angels: *"Work is through!"*

VI. OBEDIENCE PERSONIFIED

11. **Unblinking Devotion**

(Qur'an 66:6, Tafsīr Al-Jalālayn)

No tremor in the lip that seals the Horn,
No question why the End is yet unborn.
"I wait," his essence hums in cosmic night,
*"Till *Al-Malik* commands the Blast of Light."*

12. The Weight of Eternity

(Ḥadīth: "He feels not Time's weight," Shu'ab al-Īmān 1/137)

Millenniums pass like seconds in his mind,
No weariness in limbs to Time consigned.
Patience deeper than black holes' embrace—
Perfect stillness serving Perfect Grace.

VII. REVELATION'S CARRIER

13. To Mūsā at Tūr

(Qur'an 7:143, Tafsīr Al-Qummī)

When Sinai split in sacred dread,
Isrāfīl bore words that raised the dead:
"These Tablets forged in Truth's white fire—
Take them! Lift your people higher!"

14. Bearer of Final Warning

(Qur'an 78:18, 50:20)

To every prophet, his trumpet's echo came:
"Prepare your flocks for the Blast of Final Shame!"
Revelation's shadow in each divine text—
The Horn's dread note, the soul's next test.

15. Eternal Readiness

(Qur'an 16:50, Tafsīr Al-Rāzī)

Not one atom's weight of pride,
No haste, no pause at the Throne's side.
*"My breath is *Kun!* My will: *Fa Yakūn!*—*
A waiting sigh till worlds are done.

WHY HE NEVER WAVERED

"How could the Echo fight the Voice's cry?
How could the Breath resist the Sigh?
*His being is but *Amr's* vibration—*
No self exists, only pure prostration!
*Not 'angel'—but *Allāh's Decree made sound*—*
A horn that knows no will but Bound."

Rumi's Signature Style:

- Ecstatic Repetition: *"Yā Nāfikh fī'ṣ-Ṣūr!"* (O Blower of the Horn!)

- Cosmic Imagery: *"Hair of frozen lightning," "Wings like unraveling time"*

- Divine Paradox: *"Silent thunder," "Motionless vigilance"*

- Sensory Overload: *"Scent of ozone before lightning," "Taste of void on the Horn"*

- Thematic Unity: Isrāfīl as *"The Breath of Al-Qayyūm's Ultimate Command."*

"O soul asleep in Time's false night!
Be Isrāfīl's breath—*ready for the Light!*
For when the *"Blow!"* shatters space and sea,
*Only those who lived *'Amr'* shall be free.*"

***All perfection belongs to Allāh; flaws are mine. May these verses awaken us to the Final Trumpet's nearness.**

12 The Trumpet (As-Sur) – From Silence to Resurrection

(In the style of Rumi, rooted in Quran & Authentic Hadith)

---

1. The Trumpet's Creation

Before Adam's clay, before time's tide,
Allah forged the Horn where angels hide.
A spiral of light, a breath held tight—
Waiting for the Command to shatter night.
"And the Trumpet will be blown—that is the Day of Threat." (Quran 50:20)

---

2. Israfil's Vigil

His lips hover, trembling, near the golden rim,
Eyes fixed on the Throne—waiting for Him.
Millennia pass, yet he dares not blink,
For one breath could make the cosmos sink.
(Hadith: "Israfil holds the Trumpet, awaiting Allah's Order." – Tirmidhi)

---

3. The First Blow – Annihilation

"ONE!" - The Horn's cry cracks the sky's spine,
Mountains dissolve like salt in wine.
Stars scream, oceans boil to steam,
And every soul forgets its dream.
"When the Horn is blown with a single blast... the earth and mountains will be lifted and crushed with one blow." (Quran 69:13-14)

---

4. The Silence After

Forty? Years? Time is slain,
Only Allah lives—no “where,” no “when.”
No angel’s wing, no devil’s moan,
Just He on the Throne—utterly Alone.
(Hadith: “Between the two Blows is forty.” Some said 40 days, others 40 years. – Sahih Muslim)

---

5. The Second Blow – Resurrection

“TWO!” - From atoms to flesh, bones rise,
Graves burst open like butterflies.
Adam’s dust wakes, blinking, dazed—
“Was my death just a nap?” they say, amazed.
"Then it will be blown again, and behold—they will stand, gazing!" (Quran 39:68)

---

6. The Trumpet’s Echo in the Womb

Every child who died in birth,
Every buried, every burned—
Now whole again, their voices surge,
Singing the Names that all things serve.
"Not a single soul is wronged on that Day." (Quran 20:112)

---

7. The Deaf Hear It

Those who mocked, *"When will this be?"*
Now tremble as the Sound floods seas.
No earplugs, no tombs so deep,
The Trumpet mines souls from their sleep.
"No soul can hide from it." (Quran 20:108)

---

8. The Trumpet's Weight

Heavier than galaxies, yet light as a sigh,
It balances justice where all secrets lie.
Every tyrant's whip, every orphan's tear,
Now trembles in the Horn's atmosphere.

(Hadith: "The Scale will weigh deeds lighter than an atom." – Muslim)

---

9. The Animals' Judgment

Lions, lambs—all beasts shall meet,
Horns and hooves kneel at His Feet.
"Now take your vengeance!" the Command will sound,
Till claw and fang settle their ground.

(Hadith: "Animals will retaliate against each other till justice is served." – Tirmidhi)

---

10. The Sun's Nearness

A mile above, it drips despair,
Melting brows of those who didn't care.
Yet the righteous walk in gardens cool,
Their sweat perfume, their faces jeweled.

"The sun will come near, scalding heads." (Quran 70:8, Hadith – Bukhari)*

---

11. The Trumpet's Third Blow?

Some say a third for Gathering's call,
To march to Judgment where none stand tall.
Yet the Horn's final note is Mercy's own—
A mother's whisper to bring her children home.

(Scholars debate a third blast based on Quran 27:87 & Hadith variants)

---

12. The Book's Flight

Scrolls soar from angels' hands,
Some caught by joy, some burned by brands.
Left or right? The Trumpet's sound
Already wrote each soul's rebound.

***"Read your book! Your own self is sufficient as a reckoner against you this Day."* (Quran 17:14)**

---

13. The Bridge Over Hell

Thinner than hair, sharper than knives—
Some sprint like light, some crawl with lives
Weighed by sins that snag their feet,
Till the Prophet's light guides the meek.

(Hadith: "The Sirat Bridge is darker than night; believers cross like lightning." – Muslim)

---

14. The Trumpet's Final Breath

When Judgment ends, and Hell's gates close,
The Horn exhales—a rosebud grows.
New heavens bloom, new earths arise,
And Time itself kneels, realizing: **"This was always Paradise."**

***"And Paradise will be brought near to the righteous."* (Quran 26:90)**

15. The Prophets' Assembly

Muhammad (ﷺ) leads them, a banner unfurled,
Each prophet holds scrolls that once shook the world.
"Bear witness!" Allah commands—their reply:
"They heard our call, yet chose to deny."

(Quran 7:6 - "We shall question those to whom messengers were sent...")

---

16. The Sinner's Bargain

"Send me back!" the miser cries,
"I'll pray, I'll give, I'll moralize!"
But the Horn's echo laughs in return:
"You had dawns enough—now in Hellfire burn."

(Quran 23:99-100 - "Until when death comes to one of them, he says: 'My Lord, send me back...'")

---

17. The Martyrs' Ecstasy

Their necks still wet with blood's last kiss,
Now rise laughing at the Abyss.
*"Was the sword's bite all you'd give?
Jannah's wine makes death a sieve!"*
(Hadith: "Martyrs feel their wounds as fragrance." - Ahmad)

---

18. The Disbeliever's Epiphany

Pharaoh kneels, Nimrod weeps,
As the Horn's truth no veil now keeps.
*"You worshipped Self, now meet your King—
Hell's chains await your final bowing."*
(Quran 40:60 - "Indeed, those who disdain My worship will enter Hell humiliated.")

---

19. The Children's Innocence

Stillborn babes, toddlers pure,
Cluster like pearls at Judgment's door.
"Enter My Garden," the Compassionate calls,
"Your parents' tears will be your walls."
(Hadith: "Children lead their parents to Paradise." - Ahmad)

---

20. The Scholar's Ink Transfigured

Words he taught in life's brief day,
Now blaze like suns to light his way.
Each student's prayer becomes a stair—
While those who hoarded knowledge despair.
(Hadith: "The scholar's ink outweighs a martyr's blood." - Ibn Majah)

---

21. The Earth's Confession

*"O Lord! They trod me with pride and sin,
Burying orphans, hoarding tin!"*
Mountains echo: *"We restrained quakes
Only for Your forbearance's sake."*
(Quran 99:4 - "That Day, the earth will report its news.")

---

22. The Body's Testimony

Hands scream: *"We stole!"
Feet wail: *"We ran to evil's goal!"*
Tongues convulse: *"We lied!"*—
Till the Trumpet silences their tide.
(Quran 24:24 - "On the Day when their tongues, hands, and feet testify against them...")

23. The Hypocrite's Duality

Two faces worn in life's bazaar,
Now split apart like rotten star.
"Where is your cunning now?" Truth demands,
As Hell's maw gapes where his duplicity stands.
(Quran 4:145 - "Indeed, the hypocrites will be in the lowest depth of the Fire.")

---

24. The Parent's Regret

"My children! Why did you not obey?"
They snarl back: *"You taught us to stray!"*
A cycle of blame, a serpent's bite—
While the righteous families bask in light.
(Quran 80:34-36 - "That Day a man will flee from his brother, his mother, his father...")

---

25. The Trumpet's Cosmic Scale

Bigger than supernovas, yet weighing a sigh,
It measures the butterfly's altruistic flight.
Black holes kneel before its might—
What then of man who ignored the Right?
(Quran 21:47 - "We will set up scales of justice on the Day of Resurrection...")

---

26. The Angels' Awe

Millions of wings freeze mid-flutter,
As the Horn's vibration makes matter stutter.
"SubhanAllah!" their chorus rings,
While galaxies unravel like old strings.
(Quran 39:75 - "And you will see the angels surrounding the Throne, exalting their Lord...")

27. The Repenter's Joy

A thief who wept before his last breath,
Now watches angels erase his death.
*"Your tears washed the scroll clean—
Step forth! No past, no 'might have been.'"*
(Hadith Qudsi: "My mercy precedes My wrath." - Bukhari)

---

28. The Oppressor's Reckoning

Kings who built towers of broken spines,
Now beg: *"Melt us into gold mines!"*
Their victims smile, holding scales—
"Taste what your oppression entails."
(Quran 2:166 - "When those who were followed disown their followers...")

---

29. The Animals' Reckoning

A sparrow pecks the miser's eyes,
"You starved me though crumbs were your guise!"
Lions lick martyrs' feet like cubs—
All creatures settle love's or grudges' rubs.
(Hadith: "A woman entered Hell for starving a cat." - Bukhari)

---

30. The Trumpet's Final Secret

After Hell's gates are sealed with fire,
After the Saved reach their desire,
The Horn whispers to cosmic dust:
"Allah was Just—and Love was the thrust."
(Quran 11:106-107 - "As for those who are wretched... but the blessed will be in Paradise...")

---

31. The Intercession

Muhammad (ﷺ) prostrates at the Throne's base,
"Ummati! My Ummati!" tears trace.
Allah smiles: *"Raise your noble head—
Your lovers are saved, as I promised you said."*
(Hadith: "My intercession is for those who committed major sins in my Ummah." - Tirmidhi)

32. The Eternal Meeting

Face to Face—no veil, no sun,
Just He and the perfected one.
"Where is the Horn now?" the soul will sigh,
Lost in the Depth of the Loved One's Eye.
(Quran 75:22-23 - "Some faces that Day will be radiant, looking at their Lord.")

---

33. The Trumpet Becomes a Flower

Its work complete, its sound now stilled,
The Horn transforms—its curves refilled
With rivers of wine that never inebriate,
A relic in Paradise where time dissipates.

(Hadith: "Allah will create new creations as He wills." - Muslim)

Final Reflection:

The Trumpet isn't mere doom—it's the ultimate mercy call,
Separating Truth's lovers from those who chose the Fall.
Let its echo haunt your complacent nights,
And polish your soul for the First Light's sight.

Key Sources for Seekers:

1 Surah An-Nazi'at (79:6-14)* – The Two Blows
2 Surah Ya-Sin (36:51)* – "It will only be one shout..."
3 Hadith Qudsi (Divine descriptions of the Hour)
4 Surah Az-Zumar (39:68-75)* – The Two Blows in detail
5 Surah Qaf (50:20-22)* – The Trumpet's inevitability
6 Hadith of the Horn's Length* (Tirmidhi) – "Its mouth is as wide as the heavens and earth..."
7 Tafsir Ibn Kathir* – Cosmic events of Judgment Day

13 Rumi-inspired poems illuminating the creation and mission of Malak al-Mawt (Angel of Death), meticulously crafted from the Qur'an and authenticated Ḥadīth:

I. BIRTH FROM DIVINE DARKNESS

1. The Unseen Command

(Ḥadīth Qudsī, Tafsīr Ibn Kathīr 32:11)
Before life's first breath stirred the dust,
Allāh whispered: *"Death is a must."*
From *Barzakh*'s shadow, *'Amr* took form—
Malak al-Mawt! Born of the Unseen Storm.
Not light, not fire—but Absence's art,
To sever soul from fleshly heart.

2. Garments of Finality

(Ṣaḥīḥ Bukhārī 7439, Muslim 2872)
His cloak: woven from departed sighs,
His crown: extinguished stars in midnight skies.
Wings of silence—vast and deep—
Where eternal secrets sleep.

II. FORMIDABLE STATURE

3. Four Faces of Transition

(Tafsīr Al-Qurṭubī 50:19, Musnad Aḥmad 18560)
East: Joy for souls who loved their Lord,
West: Terror for rebels' last reward,
North: Mercy's call to penitent breath,
South: Justice's ice for evil's death.

4. Eyes of Dual Truths

(Ṣaḥīḥ Muslim 2872)

Right eye: Gentle as a mother's kiss,
Left eye: Lightning's consuming hiss.
For believers—peace in his gaze,
For tyrants—hell's unblinking blaze.

III. THE SOUL-TAKER

5. Hands of Destiny

(Qur'an 6:61, Tafsīr Ṭabarī)

One hand holds gentleness—rose-petal soft,
One hand grips judgment—cold and aloft.
"Come, O soul at peace!" he'll croon,
"Rebel! Your time ends—too soon!"

6. The Extraction

(Qur'an 56:83-87, Ṣaḥīḥ Bukhārī 6509)

Like silk drawn from a thorny stem—
Saints soar as he reclaims their gem.
Like roots ripped from cursed earth—
Sinners scream at their devalued worth.

IV. OBEDIENCE UNWAVERING

7. No Delay, No Advance

(Qur'an 7:34, Ṣaḥīḥ Muslim 2659)

When Pharaoh roared: *"More time! Reprieve!"*
His blade fell swift—no pause, no leave.
When prophets wept: "Let harvests grow!"
*He came—as *Al-Qadr* willed it so.*

8. The Sūrat al-Mulk Shield

(Ṣaḥīḥ Tirmidhī 2890, Ibn Mājah 3786)
For those who sought its nightly guard,
His grip grew tender, mercy-starred.
*"Recite *Al-Mulk*?"*—his voice would sigh—
"Then taste death like a lullaby."

V. DAILY DUTY

9. Leaves from the Cosmic Tree

(Ṣaḥīḥ Bukhārī 3119, 6419)
Each dawn, a tree with leaves appears—
Names of those ending earthly years.
He plucks no leaf before its hour—
Perfect servant of Divine Power.

10. Army of Assistants

(Tafsīr Ibn 'Abbās 79:1-2)
Billions of helpers—veiled, unseen—
For plague or babe in womb serene.
One soul's thread cut—his command alone—
Though helpers reap what he has sown.

VI. DIVINE MERCY & JUSTICE

11. The Repentant's Welcome

(Qur'an 4:18, Ṣaḥīḥ Muslim 2687)
When sinners gasp their final *Tawbah*,
His eyes shed light, not wrath's ardor.
"Allāh forgives!" his whisper blooms—
Transforming tombs to mercy's rooms.

12. Eternal Surrender

(Qur'an 16:50, Tafsīr Al-Jalālayn)

No pride in power, no pause, no plea—
Death's Angel serves *Al-Ḥayy*'s decree.
*"My will? *Fa Yakūn!*—Your Command is me!"*
*First and last in *Qadar*'s vast sea.*

WHY HE NEVER WAVERED

"How could the Scissor refuse the Weaver's thread?
How could the Night resist the Dawn's spread?
*His hand is but *Al-Qadr*'s own knife—*
Severing the illusion called 'life'!
*Not 'angel'—but *Allāh's Decree made manifest*—*
A servant flawless in the Ultimate Test."

Rumi's Signature Style:

- Ecstatic Paradox: *"Terror in his left gaze, lullabies in his right!"*
- Vivid Imagery: *"Garments of departed sighs," "Throne-shadowed wings"*
- Divine Resonance: *"Every death is *Bismillāh* written in blood and breath"*
- Sensory Depth: *"Scent of grave-soil," "Silence before the soul-snatch"*
- Thematic Unity: Malak al-Mawt as *"The Ultimate Surrender to Al-Mumīt (The Bringer of Death)."*

"O soul clinging to this fleeting spark.
Be like Death's Angel—*live in the Dark!*
For when he comes with *Qadar*'s scroll,
Only those who surrendered whole
Shall smile at his approach, and rise—
Born anew in the Light of the Most Wise."

All perfection is Allāh's; errors are mine. May these verses awaken us to life's true end.

14 Rumi-inspired poems illuminating the creation and eternal service of Ridwān (رضوان), Keeper of Paradise, woven from authentic Islamic sources:

1. The Genesis of Joy

(Ḥadīth: "Paradise was created from light," Musnad Aḥmad 3712)
Before Time's womb held joy or tears,
Allāh breathed: *"Bloom, Garden beyond years!"*
From Light's pure core—no clay, no flame—
Ridwān! First guardian of the Unseen Name.
His essence: Mercy's crystallized perfume,
His birth: Eternity's first bloom.
\---

2. Keys of Dawn

(Qur'an 38:50, Ṣaḥīḥ Bukhārī 3257)
Allāh swt forged eight keys from Eden's sun,
Placed in his palm—the Gatekeeper won!
Emerald shafts with diamond teeth—
"Open when souls outrun death's heath!"
\---

3. Robes of Eternal Spring

(Tafsīr Ibn Kathīr 76:12-22)
His cloak: woven from jasmine rains,
Stitched with threads where *houris* dance.
Scent of musk from Kāfūr's stream—
A living robe of Mercy's dream.
\---

4. Face of Welcoming

(Qur'an 13:24, Ṣaḥīḥ Muslim 2831)
Two eyes: deep as Firdaws' lakes,
Where martyrs drink what thirst forsakes.
Smile like crescent moons that rise—
"Salām! O pure! Claim your prize!"

5. The Gatekeeper's Oath

(Ḥadīth Qudsī: "I prepare what no eye has seen," Bukhārī 7498)
At the Throne, he knelt and swore:
*"No unworthy soul shall pass this door!
I'll guard Your Secrets, lush and deep—
Till the faithful from the *Ṣirāṭ* leap!"*
*Allāh smiled: *"Ridwān! Lift your gaze—*
Your name shall crown My Mercy's ways."

6. Judgment Day Vigil

(Qur'an 89:27-30, Ṣaḥīḥ Muslim 2870)
When Hell howls *"More!"* with famished jaw,
He stands serene at Heaven's law.
Scrolls in hand, he calls the blest—
"Enter where no soul's oppressed!"

7. The Martyr's Welcome

(Ṣaḥīḥ Muslim 1887, Tirmidhī 1661)
For those who fell on war's red field,
He spreads green silk where wounds are healed.
"Allāh greets you!" his voice cascades—*
Crimson dust to emerald shades.

8. Obedience Unshaken

(Qur'an 16:50, Tafsīr Al-Qurṭubī)
When Iblīs begged: *"Let me peek inside!"*
His keys flashed *"No!"* like lightning's pride.
"Not for worlds," his whisper burned—*
*"Only whom *Al-Ghafūr* earned!"*

9. The Humble Gate-Sweeper

(Ḥadīth: "Angels polish Paradise with wings," Ṣaḥīḥ Ibn Ḥibbān)

Each dawn, he dusts the pearl gates' sheen,
Though Heaven's Keeper, humble, keen.
"How dare I boast?" he sighs to streams—*
"I'm but dust in Mercy's dreams."

---

10. Eternal Chorus

(Qur'an 56:25-26, Ṣaḥīḥ Bukhārī 3245)

No word but *"Salām!"* rings in his domain,
No wish unmet, no lingering pain.
He stands where Light meets Light's own Source—
First welcome to the Soul's true Course.

WHY HE NEVER WAVERED

"How could the Door defy the House's King?
How could the Stream shun the Ocean-Spring?
*His keys are but *Al-Jalīl*'s decree—*
*No will exists but *"Allāh wills for me!"*
*Not 'angel'—but *Ar-Raḥmān's Welcome made form*—*
A threshold where the faithful storm."

Rumi's Signature Style:

- Ecstatic Repetition: *"Salām! Salām! Salām!"* echoing through gates
- Nature Metaphors: *"Keys like dawn," "Robes of jasmine rains"*
- Divine Paradox: *"Keeper of Glory, sweeper of floors"*
- Sensory Richness: *"Scent of Kāfūr," "Emerald light," "Silk of martyrs' peace"*
- Thematic Unity: Ridwān as *"The Embodied Yes of Divine Mercy."*

"O soul! Be Ridwān's key—unlock the Real!
Guard your heart's gate from false and frail!
For when Death's angel whispers *'Come!'*
*His *Salām* shall greet you—Kingdom won.*"

***All perfection belongs to Allāh; flaws are mine. May these verses draw us toward the Gates of Eternal peace.**

15 Rumi-inspired poems on Malik (مَالِك), Warden of Jahannam, meticulously crafted from Quranic verses and authenticated Ḥadīth:

1. Genesis of Divine Wrath

(Qur'an 43:77, Ḥadīth Qudsī)

Before Hell's pits were dug in endless night,
Allāh forged Malik from Sacred Might—
Not fire like jinn, but Wrath's pure core,
A keeper for the souls Mercy ignored.
"Guard My Justice!" thundered the Command.
*He bowed: *"Your Decree is my only stand."*

2. Formed of Liquid Regret

(Tafsīr Ibn Kathīr 40:49, Ṣaḥīḥ Muslim 2847)

His skin: blackened chains of sinners' sighs,
His eyes: volcanoes where lost hope lies.
No pupil gleams—just ember-glow,
Watching depths no light can know.

---

3. The Reluctant Tormentor

(Qur'an 74:30-31, Ṣaḥīḥ Bukhārī 7439)

Nineteen thousand Zabāniyah at his call,
Yet grief cracks his voice: *"Must they all fall?*
O Rabb! Must I scorch the child of Ādam's clay?"
*But obeys when *Amr* says: *"Burn them today!"*

4. Crown of Frozen Screams

(Ḥadīth: "His face reflects Jahannam's pain," Musnad Aḥmad 18834)

Upon his head—a crown of ice and flame,
Each spike a curse, each gem a shard of shame.
"You ruled with pride?" its thorns declare,
"Now rule this hell your deeds prepared!"

5. The Gates of Despair

(Qur'an 39:71-72, Tafsīr Ṭabarī)
Seven gates he guards with keys of dread—
Saqar for liars, *Ḥāwiyah* for the misled.
"Enter!" his growl makes mountains weep,
"Your laughter's ash, your sins run deep."
---

6. Mercy in Obedience

(Qur'an 6:12, Ṣaḥīḥ Muslim 2847)
When a believer's kin scream in the blaze,
He whispers: *"Had you walked His ways..."*
Tears of acid scar his cheek—
Yet never spares the weak.
---

7. Keeper of the Ledger

(Qur'an 18:49, Tafsīr Al-Qurṭubī)
In hands of smoke, he holds the Scroll of Loss—
Each page a sin, each line a broken cross.
"Taste what your hands designed!" he roars,
As justice locks eternal doors.
---

8. The Weight of Eternity

(Ḥadīth: "He never smiles," Ṣaḥīḥ Bukhārī 4850)
Since time began, no joy has touched his face,
No rest from wrath in this forsaken place.
"Smile?" he rasps. *"How could I dare,*
When rebels choke on their own despair?"

9. Judgment Day's Cry

(Qur'an 89:23-24, Ṣaḥīḥ Muslim 2847)

When Jahannam groans: *"Are there more to burn?"*
He pleads: *"O Rabb! Let my vigil adjourn!"*
*But Allāh's Voice: *"Stand firm, Malik!*
Till Justice drinks its final drip."

10. The Unbroken Servant

(Qur'an 66:6, Tafsīr Ibn 'Abbās)

Not once his will defied the Throne's decree,
No pity stayed his hand—though shattered be.
"Flame am I," he sighs through smoke,
*"Kindled only when *Al-Ḥaqq* spoke."*

WHY HE NEVER WAVERED

"How could the Scorcher refuse the Flame?
How could the Judge distort the Claim?
*His wrath is but *Al-'Adl*'s fierce face—*
No heart to spare, no pause, no grace.
*Not 'tormentor'—but *Allāh's Justice made fire*—*
*A mirror to the damned: *'You chose this pyre!'"*

Rumi's Signature Style:

- Stark Imagery: *"Crown of frozen screams," "Skin of sinners' sighs"*
- Divine Paradox: *"Weeping while burning," "Reluctant wrath"*
- Rhythmic Intensity: *Jahannam's gates clanging through verses*
- Theological Depth: Malik as *"The Unflinching Hand of Al-Muntaqim (The Avenger)."*
- Sensory Overload: *"Acid tears," "Chains of regret," "Scorched scrolls"*

"O soul! Be Malik's warning—not his guest!
Let hell's dread echo break your earthly rest!
For Justice waits beyond death's thin disguise...
Repent!—before you meet his weeping eyes."

All perfection belongs to Allāh; errors are mine. May these verses awaken us to the Reality of Divine Justice.

16 Rumi-inspired poems on the Kirām al-Kātibīn (Noble Recorders), crafted from authentic Quranic verses and Ḥadīth, illuminating their creation, obedience, and eternal mission:

1. Genesis of the Witnesses

(Qur'an 82:10–12, Ṣaḥīḥ Muslim 2996)
Before Adam's clay drew breath,
Light split into two—*life and death*:
Kirām al-Kātibīn! Born of *Nūr's* decree,
Twin scribes for every soul set free.
No pause, no sleep, no mortal sight—
Eyes peeled through eternal night.

2. Shoulder-Sentinels

(Qur'an 50:17–18, Ṣaḥīḥ Tirmidhī 369)
Right: Quill of sunbeam, scroll of dawn,
Left: Ink of shadow, parchment drawn.
One records the mercy-seed,
One etches every selfish greed.
No blink, no breath—ceaseless gaze,
Guardians of life's fleeting maze.

3. Feathers of Divine Decree

(Tafsīr Ibn Kathīr 82:11, Ṣaḥīḥ Bukhārī 6509)
Wings like comets, silent, vast—
Each plume a future, present, past.
Feathers dipped in cosmic ink,
*Writing *Qadar* before souls blink.*

4. Inkwells of Eternity

(Ḥadīth Qudsī: "Pen dried, fate sealed," Tirmidhī 2156)
Their ink: distilled from *Al-Lawḥ's* light,
Black for sin, gold for right.
*No drop spilled without *Amr's* nod—*
Scripting truth by will of God.

5. The Whisper Registry

(Qur'an 43:80, Ṣaḥīḥ Muslim 6844)
Hear their quills scratch night and noon—
"That hidden grudge... this orphan's boon..."
Even thoughts like scattered moths,
Trapped in ink, spared not, forgot.

6. Mercy in Du'ā's Ink

(Ṣaḥīḥ Ibn Ḥibbān 870, Qur'an 40:60)
When tears stain the sinner's sheet,
The right-hand angel writes *sweet*:
"Repentance blooms!"—his quill aflame,
Erasing blots in Allāh's name.

7. Bathroom Vigil's Pause

(Ṣaḥīḥ Abū Dāwūd 4019, Tirmidhī 606)
At ablution's sacred door,
They lift their pens—record no more.
"Privacy!" Mercy's shield descends—
No shame exposed where grace defends.

8. The Humble Invisibility

(Ṣaḥīḥ Muslim 2996, Tafsīr Al-Qurṭubī)
Unseen, unheard—yet nearer than veins,
Veiled like rain on drought-struck plains.
No boast, no form, no earthly trace—
Silent witnesses to the soul's race.

9. Judgment Day Testimony

(Qur'an 69:19–20, Ṣaḥīḥ Bukhārī 4935)
When books fly open, scorched or bright,
They'll cry: *"We wrote by day and night!*
No word missed—no secret plea!"
Sealing fates for all to see.

10. Eternal Surrender

(Qur'an 16:50, 66:6)

Not one sigh strays from *Amr's* thread,
No question why the damned are dead.
*"We are but *Qalam* in Your Hand—*
*Writing *'Kun!'* at Your command!"*

WHY THEY NEVER SWAYED

"How could the Pen defy the Writer's will?
How could the Ink refuse the Page to fill?
*Their essence is but *Al-Ḥaqq*'s decree—*
*No 'self' exists, only *'Allāh wills for me!'*
*Not scribes—but *Al-'Alīm's* seeing hand,*
Writing what the soul could not understand."

Rumi's Signature Style:

- Ecstatic Paradox: *"Unseen yet nearer than breath!"*
- Light Metaphors:*"Quills of comet-fire," "Ink of cosmic night"*
- Divine Intimacy: *"Shoulder-angels closer than lovers"*
- Rhythmic Witness: *Scratch of pens echoing through poems*
- Thematic Unity: Angels as *"The Ever-Obedient Ink of Al-Qadr."*

"O soul! Be their parchment—pure and bright!
Let every deed reflect the *Nūr*'s true light!
For when the books fly open wide,
Your script will blaze where truths reside."

All perfection belongs to Allāh; errors are mine. May these verses remind us we are eternally witnessed.

17 Rumi-inspired poems illuminating Rāqib & ʿAtīd (The Vigilant Watchers), meticulously crafted from Qur'anic verses and authenticated Ḥadīth, revealing their divine purpose and unwavering obedience:

1. Birth of the Witnesses

(Qur'an 50:18, Ṣaḥīḥ Muslim 2996)
Before Adam's lungs drew earthly air,
Twin flames of Light burned beyond compare:
Rāqib! ʿAtīd! Forged from *Nūr's* command—
Eternal scribes for every soul's strand.
No sleep, no blink—their gaze holds fast,
Recording deeds from first to last.

2. Shoulder-Sentinels

(Qur'an 82:10-12, Tafsīr Ibn Kathīr)
Right: Rāqib's quill of molten gold,
Left: ʿAtīd's ink of shadows cold.
One scroll gleams where mercy flows,
One darkens where rebellion grows.
No word escapes—no thought takes flight—
Truth's ledger burns through day and night.

3. Eyes of Cosmic Clarity

(Ṣaḥīḥ Bukhārī 6509, Qur'an 43:80)
Four orbs that pierce illusion's veil:
Two see the deed, two trace intent's trail.
Right eye: Dawn's unerring grace,
Left eye: Midnight's judgment-face.

4. Wings of Unceasing Vigil

(Tafsīr Al-Qurṭubī 13:11, Ṣaḥīḥ Muslim 6844)
Feathers like comets—silent, vast—
Archiving futures, presents, pasts.
One flap: a lifetime's breaths inscribed,
No secret in the soul can hide.

5. Inkwells of Divine Decree

(Ḥadīth Qudsī: "Pen dried, fate sealed," Tirmidhī 2156)
Their ink: distilled from *Al-Lawḥ's* stream—
Gold for hope, black for envy's scream.
*Not a drop spills without *Amr's* nod,*
*Writing *Qadar* by will of God.*

6. The Whisper Chronicles

(Qur'an 54:52-53, Ṣaḥīḥ Muslim 6844)
Hear quills scratch in the heart's deep night:
"That hidden grudge... this prayer's light..."
Even breath that shapes no sound,
In their scrolls is tightly bound.
---

7. Mercy in the Margins

(Ṣaḥīḥ Ibn Ḥibbān 870, Qur'an 4:110)
When tears drown sins in repentance's rain,
Rāqib's** gold quill purifies the stain.
"Tawbah blooms!"—his script aflame,*
Erasing blots in Allāh's name.

8. Bathroom Vigil's Pause

(Ṣaḥīḥ Abū Dāwūd 4019, Tirmidhī 606)
At the privy's humble door,
Lifted pens record no more.
"Privacy's grace!"—a mercy-shield,*
Where shame is veiled, no sin revealed.

9. Judgment Day Testimony

(Qur'an 69:19-20, Ṣaḥīḥ Bukhārī 4935)
When books fly open—dark or bright—
They'll cry: *"We wrote by day and night!*
No atom's weight escaped our sight!"
Sealing fates in piercing light.

10. Eternal Surrender

(Qur'an 16:50, 66:6)

Not one breath strays from *Amr's* thread,
No question why the damned are dead.
*"We are but *Qalam* in Your Hand—*
*Writing *'Kun!'* at Your command!"*

WHY THEY NEVER SWAYED

"How could the Pen resist the Writer's will?
How could the Ink refuse the Page to fill?
*Their essence is but *Al-Ḥaqq*'s decree—*
*No 'self' exists, only *'Allāh wills through me!'*
*Not watchers—but *As-Samīʿ's* hearing ear,*
Writing what the soul could not hide or veer."

Rumi's Signature Style:

- Ecstatic Paradox: *"Silent yet writing every sound!"*
- Light/Dark Imagery: *"Quills of comet-fire," "Ink of cosmic shadows"*
- Divine Intimacy: *"Closer than breath, farther than stars"*
- Rhythmic Witness: *Scratch of pens echoing through verses*
- Thematic Unity: Angels as *"The Ever-Present Ink of Al-Ḥafīẓ (The Preserver)."*

"O soul! Be their parchment—pure and bright!
Let your deeds reflect the *Nūr*'s true light!
For when the books fly open wide,
Your script will blaze where truths reside."

All perfection belongs to Allāh; errors are mine. May these verses remind us we are eternally witnessed.

18 Rumi-inspired poems on the angels Munkar & Nakīr (The Grave Interrogators), meticulously crafted from Qur'anic principles and authenticated Ḥadīth, revealing their divine purpose and unyielding obedience:

1. Genesis of the Grave's Inquisitors

(Ḥadīth: "Allāh creates angels from light," Ṣaḥīḥ Muslim 2996)
From *Nūr's* core where shadows fear to tread,
Twin flames of Truth—**Munkar & Nakīr!**—were bred.
Not clay, nor fire, but Judgment's purest ray,
Forged to test the soul on its final day.
"Question all!" the Throne's command rang clear—
"Let no lie escape the grave's dark sphere."

2. Forms That Shatter Night

(Ḥadīth: "Blue-black, with eyes like lightning," Sunan Abī Dāwūd 4753)
Skin like midnight storms where thunders brood,
Eyes like comets—scorching, raw, and rude.
Munkar's voice: Earthquakes torn asunder,
Nakīr's gaze: Stars ripped in wonder.
No mortal flesh could bear their sight—
Pure terror cloaked in holy light.

3. The Grave's Unblinking Tribunal

(Ḥadīth: "They ask three questions," Ṣaḥīḥ al-Jāmiʿ 1676)
When earth seals tight its earthen door,
They stand as Truth's unflinching core:
"Who is your Lord? What is your faith?
Who is this Prophet beyond life and death?"
No pause, no hint—their query stark—
Lightning splitting the grave's cold dark.

4. Instruments of Divine Decree

(Qur'an 6:61, Tafsīr Ibn Kathīr)

No wrath of their own, no vengeful hand—
They execute what *Al-Ḥaqq* has planned.
For believers: faces soften as dawn,
For liars: hammers shattering bone.
"Mercy or wrath?" they do not choose—
*Only *Amr's* iron path they use.*

5. The Sinner's Torment

(Ḥadīth: "The grave tightens," Ṣaḥīḥ al-Bukhārī 1379)

When rebels choke on hollow lies,
Their clubs ignite with hellfire cries:
"Taste denial's fruit!"—each blow descends,
*Till *Barzakh's* night with anguish rends.*
*No blow struck but by *Qadar's* design,*
No pain unleashed but the Divine.

6. The Believer's Peace

(Ḥadīth: "The grave widens," Ṣaḥīḥ Muslim 2870)

For souls who whisper *"Lā ilāha,"* true,
Their eyes gleam gardens drenched in dew:
"Sleep in light!" their voices croon—
A lullaby beneath the moon.
"Your Lord smiles!"—their clubs now bloom*
As roses scattering sweet perfume.

7. Unseen Yet Omnipresent

(Qur'an 13:11, Tafsīr Al-Qurṭubī)

No grave too deep, no tomb forgot,
No prince or pauper spared their lot.
They pierce mountains, oceans, sand—
*Guided by *Al-ʿAlīm's* command.*
East to West, their wings expand—
Death's relentless, silent band.

8. Obedience Like Mountains*

(Qur'an 16:50, Ḥadīth Qudsī)
When Iblīs hissed: *"Spare this king!"*
Their clubs fell swift—no faltering.
*"We serve none but *Al-Malik*!"* they roared,*
Crushing the plea hell's minions poured.
*Not one breath strays from *Amr's* thread—*
"Allāh decrees!"—all questions dead.*

9. The Humility of Power

(Ḥadīth: "Angels never boast," Ṣaḥīḥ Ibn Ḥibbān)
Though thrones and empires dread their tread,
Before Allāh's Throne, they bow their head:
"We are but tools—Your wrath, Your grace—
Nothing of us in this sacred space!"

10. Eternal Guardians of the In-Between

(Qur'an 3:185, Tafsīr Ṭabarī)
Till the Trumpet rends the sky apart,
They guard *Barzakh* with steadfast heart:
"No soul escapes its reckoning day—
Truth's scales await, come what may!"
*Their vigil ends when *Isrāfīl* sounds—*
*In *Al-Ḥaqq's* justice, all is found.*

WHY THEY NEVER SWAYED

"How could the Hammer shun the Anvil's call?
How could the Lightning flee the Thunder's thrall?
*Their might is but *Al-Qahhār's* breath—*
*No will exists save *'Allāh orders death!'*
*Not judges—but *Al-Ḥakam's* verdict made steel,*
*Striking where *Al-ʿAdl* decrees to heal or peel.*"

Rumi's Signature Style:

- Ecstatic Duality: *"Clubs that bloom roses or spit fire!"*
- Sensory Terror/Awe: *"Skin like cracked obsidian," "Voices like tectonic plates"*
- Divine Paradox: *"Torturers with tears of light"*
- Rhythmic Interrogation: *"Who is your Lord? What is your Deen?"* echoing
- Thematic Unity: Angels as *"The Unflinching Scalpel of Al-Mumīt (The Giver of Death)."*

"O soul! When these twins rend your tomb's dark veil,
Let *Lā ilāha* be your armor, not a wail!
For their clubs turn gentle for those who knew:
*Allāh's *Rahmah* waits beyond the interview.*"

All perfection is Allāh's; flaws are mine. May these verses awaken us to the Grave's Reality.

19 **Rumi-inspired poems on the Zabāniyya (ةَيِناَبَز), the nineteen guardians of Jahannam, meticulously crafted from Qur'anic verses and authenticated Ḥadīth:**

1. Forged in Divine Wrath

(Qur'an 74:30–31, Tafsīr Ibn Kathīr)
From Jaḥīm's core, where damned souls weep,
Nineteen flames roared from depths unseen and deep:
Zabāniyya! Scourges of the rebelling throng—
"By My Might!" declared the Throne's command strong.
Not light like Jibrīl—but hellfire's breath,
Born to execute the second death.

2. Forms of Terror

(Ḥadīth: "With hooks of iron," Ṣaḥīḥ Muslim 2847)
Skin like molten brass in eternal night,
Eyes like fissures bleeding crimson light.
Claws like scimitars forged in divine ire,
Teeth like glaciers gnashing hell's own fire.
Nineteen giants—mountain-high and vast—
Shadows where all hope is cast.

3. The Unbreakable Nineteen

(Qur'an 74:30–31, Tafsīr Al-Qurṭubī)
"Why *nineteen*?" scoffed the faithless chief—
Allāh answered: *"To magnify unbelief's grief!*
A test for man, a warning stark—
Each clawed hand leaves its eternal mark."
No more, no less—their number stands,
As fixed as stars by the Lord's commands.

4. Chains of Rebellion

(Ḥadīth: "They drag by the face," Ṣaḥīḥ Muslim 2847)
With hooks plunged deep in jawbone and soul,
They haul the arrogant toward their goal:
"Taste the fruit of your pride!" they roar,
As sinners shriek toward hell's core.
No pity moves their furnace-hearts—
*Only *Al-Jabbār's* wrath imparts.*

5. Flames of Obedience

(Qur'an 66:6, Tafsīr Al-Jalālayn)
When Pharaoh's magicians bowed in faith,
Their claws froze still, defying hell's wraith.
"Hold!" they hissed, though fire burned within—
For Mercy's decree outweighed the sin.
*Not a spark unleashed without *Amr's* call—*
Perfect servants, standing tall.

6. The Sinner's Torment

(Qur'an 22:19–22, Ṣaḥīḥ Bukhārī 7439)
Garments of boiling pitch they sew, > Force-fed thorns where faith did not grow.
*"Drink *Ḥamīm*!*" their laughter cracks—
As skin regenerates for new attacks.
*Each blow prescribed by *Al-Ḥakam's* scroll—*
Justice measured, soul by soul.

7. Subjugation to Malik

(Qur'an 43:77, Tafsīr Ṭabarī)
Before Malik, whose tears burn like lead,
They kneel and ask: *"Release the dead?"*
*He rasps: *"Forever!"*—their claws descend,*
No plea, no bargain, no amend.
Even hell's wardens bow that hour—
*All serve *Al-Malik's* flawless power.*

8. Eyes of Absolute Truth

(Ḥadīth: "No injustice this Day," Ṣaḥīḥ Muslim 2878)
Nineteen pairs of eyes—no deceit, no lie—
See the soul's worth as they pass by.
For martyrs: averted, veiled in shame,
For tyrants: delight in the scorching game.
"You chose this!" their silence screams—
*Reflecting *Al-'Adl's* perfect schemes.*

9. The Humility of Fury

(Qur'an 16:50, Ḥadīth Qudsī)
Though empires tremble at their tread,
Before the Throne, they bow their head:
"We are but sparks from Your fierce flame—
Not ours the glory, nor the blame!"
No boast, no pride in hell's domain—
*Only *Al-Qahhār's* sovereign reign.*

10. Eternity's Enforcers

(Qur'an 78:21–30, Ṣaḥīḥ Muslim 2847)
Till stars decay and time's chains sever,
Nineteen stand guard—relenting never.
"Allāh decreed!" their purpose roars—
As Jahannam hungers, howls, and soars.
Their fire burns by Divine Design—
Final proof of the Sacred Line.

WHY THEY NEVER WAVERED

"How could the Scourge resist the Scorcher's hand?
How could the Brand refuse the Burning Brand?
*Their fury is but *Al-Muntaqim's* breath—*
*No will exists but *'Allāh ordains this death!'*
*Not torturers—but *Al-Ḥaqq's* justice made flame,*
*Searing where *Al-Ḥakam* decrees the blame."*

Rumi's Signature Style:

- Ecstatic Terror *"Claws like shattered galaxies! Hooks like crescent moons of doom!"*
- Paradox: *"Fury in submission, wrath in perfect peace"*
- Sensory Onslaught: *"Scent of scorched pride," "Sound of snapping sinews," "Taste of boiling regret"*
- Refrain: *"Nineteen!"* echoing as divine warning
- Thematic Unity: Zabāniyya as *"The Unflinching Hammers of Al-Jabbār (The Compeller)."*

"O soul! When you stand before these nineteen eyes,

Let your deeds be pure, your repentance wise!

For their hooks seize only those who chose to flee—

*From the *Rahmah* of the One, the Eternal, the Free!"*

All perfection belongs to Allāh; errors are mine. May these verses awaken us to the Reality of Divine Justice.

20.Rumi-inspired poems illuminating the Ḥamalat al-‘Arsh (حَمَلَةُ الْعَرْشِ) – the Bearers of the Divine Throne – crafted from the Qur'an and authenticated Ḥadīth, with cosmic imagery and theological precision:

I. GENESIS OF THE THRONE-BEARERS

1. Primordial Command

(Ḥadīth Qudsī: "I was a Hidden Treasure," Al-Aḥadīth al-Qudsīyah)
Before Time's womb conceived a star,
Allāh whispered: *"Bear My Throne afar!"*
From *Nūr's* core, four giants awoke—
Ḥamalat al-‘Arsh! First breath Heaven spoke.
Not clay, nor fire—but light's purest stream,
Forged to uphold the Unseen Dream.

2. The First Groan

(Ṣaḥīḥ Ibn Ḥibbān: "Their groans are worship," 361)
As shoulders met the Throne's dread weight,
A sound birthed galaxies: *"Subḥānallāh!"* shook creation's gate.
Comets flinched at that primal cry—
Cosmic tasbīḥ beneath the sky.

II. COSMIC STATURE

3. Scale of the ‘Arsh

(Ṣaḥīḥ Bukhārī 4811, Tafsīr Ṭabarī)
Wider than seven heavens combined,
Deeper than black holes' starving mind.
Its height? A million years' ascent—
No angel's gaze knows its extent.

4. Bearers' Magnitude

(Tafsīr Al-Qurṭubī 69:17, Musnad Aḥmad 18560)
Each angel's foot crushes constellations,
Each eyelash shades doomed nations.
From sole to crown—fifty thousand years!
Yet beneath the Throne, they drown in tears.

III. FORM & ATTRIBUTES

5. Faces of Creation

(Ḥadīth: "Four faces," Tafsīr Ibn Kathīr 40:7)
Lion (East): Roars justice across the void,
Eagle (West): Sees where stars are destroyed,
Bull (North): Bears weight with cosmic might,
Man (South): Weeps mercy into night.

6. Wings of Eternity

(Ṣaḥīḥ Muslim 2846)
Wings like nebulae—silk and storm—
Each feather a universe taking form.
One flap: eternity's breath exhales,
Two flaps: destiny's ship sets sails.

IV. THE CARRYING

7. Posture of Awe

(Qur'an 40:7, Tafsīr Al-Bayḍāwī)
Knees bent, backs arched, veins ablaze—
Shoulders cracking under the Glorious Craze.
"Yā Ḥayy! Yā Qayyūm!" their chorus swells,*
As black holes shatter where their tread dwells.

8. Tears of Submission

(Ḥadīth: "Tears carve rivers in Heaven," Ṣaḥīḥ Ibn Mājah 4191)
Sweat like comets streaks their cheeks,
Falling as galaxies on mountain peaks.
*Each drop a hymn: *"Lā quwwata illā billāh!"*—*
Fueling creation's endless thaw.

V. JUDGMENT DAY TRANSFORMATION

9. Eight Bearers Rise

(Qur'an 69:17, Ṣaḥīḥ Tirmidhī 3317)
When Isrāfīl's trumpet rends the sky,
Four more giants join the cry:
"We bear! We break!"—their spines ignite,*
Doubled strength for the Final Light.

10. The Throne Aloft

(Ṣaḥīḥ Muslim 2846, Tafsīr Al-Jalālayn)
On Resurrection's scorching plain,
They lift the Throne through stars like rain.
"Behold your Lord!" the Bearers roar—*
Souls weep where none had wept before.

VI. OBEDIENCE UNBREAKABLE

11. No Complaint, No Pause

(Qur'an 21:20, Tafsīr Al-Rāzī)
Millenniums pass—no muscle sags,
No plea for rest, no banner brags.
"Carry!"—they press into the night,*
"Drop us?"—unthinkable in *Al-Quddūs'* sight!

12. Eternal Hymn

(Qur'an 39:75, Ṣaḥīḥ Bukhārī 7439)

"Subḥāna Dhīl-'Arshil-'Aẓīm!" they sigh,
As supernovas birth and die.
First to bow, last to rise—
*Reflecting *Al-Malik* in their eyes.*

WHY THEY NEVER BUCKLED

"How could Atlas flee the Sky He bears?
How could Rivers shun the Ocean's prayers?
*Their strength is but *Al-Jabbār's* loan—*
No will exists but His alone!
*Not giants—but *Al-'Aẓīm's* shadow made form,*
Bent in worship through the endless storm."

Rumi's Signature Style:

- Ecstatic Hyperbole: *"Tears carving galaxies! Shoulders cracking black holes!"*
- Cosmic Paradox: *"Colossal yet humble," "Groaning in ecstasy"*
- Kinetic Imagery: *"Wings birthing universes," "Veins of liquid starlight"*
- Refrain: *"Subḥānallāh!"* echoing as structural rhythm
- Theological Depth: Bearers as *"The Ultimate Symbol of Creaturely Surrender."*

"O soul! When your burdens crack your spine,
Recall these giants at the Sacred Sign!
For if they *groan* beneath *Al-'Aẓīm's* reign—
Your struggles are but mercy's sweetest rain."

All perfection belongs to Allāh; flaws are mine. May these verses lift our hearts to the Throne of Mercy.

21 Poems in the style of Rumi, grounded in authentic Islamic sources (Quran & Sahih Hadith), detailing the creation, purpose, trial, and wisdom of Harut and Marut:

1. The Divine Spark (Creation)

From Light's pure essence, before Time took flight,
Allah commanded: "Be!" Two stars ignite.
Not clay, nor fire, but radiance refined,
Harut and Marut, of the Celestial kind.
Their wings, the sigh of dawn's first gentle hue,
Their hearts, reflecting Knowledge ever true.
Created solely for His Throne's embrace,
To serve, to glorify, to seek His Grace.

2. The Whisper of Wonder (Observing Humanity)

From lofty heights, they watched mankind below,
Observing choices only mortals know.
They saw the soul's descent, the fractured will,
The good rejected, chasing pathways ill.>A question bloomed within their perfect sight:
"O Lord, why do they stray from Perfect Light?"

3. The Divine Response (The Challenge)

Allah, the All-Knowing, the All-Wise,
Heard their pure query beneath the endless skies.
"You see the surface, not the inner fight,
The soul weighed down, veiled from the Purest Light.
You judge the slip, but not the steep incline,
Nor feel the whisper of the serpent's sign."

4. The Angelic Claim (Confidence)

"O Lord!" they spoke, with certainty profound,
"Had we such form upon the earthly ground,
With knowledge given, purpose clear and bright,
We'd never falter, never seek the night!
We'd worship purely, shun the lowly way,
And keep Your Commands perfect, night and day."

5. The Divine Test Conceived (The Decree)

The All-Wise Lord, Whose Plan transcends all thought,
A test profound for these two angels wrought.
"Descend then," came the Word, decreeing fate,
"To Babylon's ancient, knowledge-laden gate.
Live as men live, feel what men feel inside,
Then see if pure obedience will abide."

6. The Descent (Entering the World)

From realms of Light to dust and mortal air,
Harut and Marut, bearing wisdom rare,
But clad in flesh, with senses newly born,
Faced earthly twilight, shadow, and the thorn.
Knowledge they kept, a trust from Heaven's store,
But now with limbs that tired, hearts that could adore... things.

7. The Lure of Beauty (First Temptation)

Then came a woman, beauty's very name,
Zuhra, whose glance could kindle hidden flame.
She sought their secret, magic's potent art,
A key they guarded deep within the heart.
"Teach me," she pleaded, "this celestial lore!"
But first, a price was asked – to sin, implore.

8. The Price of Desire (The Three Choices)

"Deny your God," she whispered, dark and low,
"Drink deep this wine, where forbidden currents flow,
Then take a life unjust, and seal the pact."
Three gates to darkness, a destructive act.
The angels recoiled, purity their plea,
"We seek refuge in Allah! This cannot be!"

9. The Inner Struggle (Free Will Engaged)

But flesh is weak, a vessel newly formed,
Where heavenly light with earthly shadow stormed.
Desire, unknown before, a subtle ache,
A thirst for beauty, for sensation's sake.
Their perfect certainty began to fray,
As mortal weakness whispered them astray.

10. The First Fall (Shirk Rejected, Wine Embraced)

Deny the Maker? Never! That they spurned,
The very thought made every conscience burned.
But weary, tempted, seeking solace deep,
They touched the wine, secrets within to keep.
"Just this," they murmured, "to forget the test,"
Yet in that sip, pure radiance was distressed.

11. The Deepening Shadow (The Second Fall)

Wine's false warmth spread, a fog upon the mind,
Reason, their birthright, now lay undermined.
Zuhra returned, her demand fierce and cold,
The murderous pact must now unfold.
Blinded by passion, judgment led astray,
An innocent soul was taken, cast away.

12. The Shattering Realization (Guilt)

As lifeblood flowed, a horror sharp and clear,
Pierced through the wine's dull, deceptive veneer.
Like shattered glass, their angelic pride lay bare,
Stained by the sin they swore they'd never dare.
"What have we done?" The cry tore through the night,
Replaced pure worship with remorseful fright.

13. The Choice of Mercy (Repentance Offered)

Allah, the Merciful, the Oft-Returning,
Offered a path, their souls from darkness spurning.
"Ascend!" The Call, a lifeline pure and bright,
Leave this dark trial, return to endless Light.
But knowing now the weight of sin's dark chain,
They saw the justice in enduring pain.

14. The Acceptance of Justice (Suspended State)

"O Lord," they wept, heads bowed in deep despair,
"Here let us hang, suspended in mid-air.
In Babylon's pit, where darkness finds its home,
Until Your Judgment Day, we shall not roam.
A sign for mortals, of temptation's snare,
And Mercy's depth beyond compare."

15. The Function of Warning (Teaching with Caution)

So in that pit, inverted, bound by grace,
They taught the secrets of that forbidden space.
But ever warning, with a solemn plea:
"We are a trial! Turn back! Seek Unity!
This magic harms, divides the soul apart,
Unless it strengthens faith within the heart."

16. The Divine Wisdom Unveiled (Purpose of the Test)

Allah decreed this trial not for their fall,
But so that angels hearken to His Call:
"Judge not mankind with pride, nor scorn their plight,
Their path is steeper, veiled from purest Light.
I test the servant, strength and weakness know,
My Mercy flows where humble hearts repentant go."

17. The Lesson of Humility (For Angels)

O lofty angels, near the Throne Divine,
See Harut, Marut, on that earthly line!
Knowledge you hold, yet understanding fails,
To grasp the soul where doubt and longing sails.
Judge not the sinner lost in error's night,
Whom Allah guides back to the Path of Light.

18. The Lesson of Vigilance (For Humanity)

O Son of Adam! See the warning clear,
In Babylon's pit, suspended, ever near!
Knowledge is trust, a double-edged bright sword,
Used for His Sake, it draws you near the Lord.
Misused for power, lust, or selfish gain,
It brings but chains of agonizing pain.

19. The Reality of Temptation

Think not the pure are safe from Satan's art,
He strikes the fortress of the guarded heart.
Desire's sweet poison, offered like a friend,
Leads step by step to a destructive end.
Harut and Marut, angels clothed in Light,
Succumbed when veiled from Heaven's piercing sight.

20. The Power of Repentance (Tawbah)

Yet mark their choice, when shattered by the sin,
To face the justice, not to hide within.
They sought no pardon shirking consequence,
Embracing penance, seeking recompense.
True Tawbah's door swings open, wide and free,
For all who turn, repentant, faithfully.

21. The Suspension: Mercy in Disguise

That hanging state, inverted, deep and cold,
Is not pure wrath, but Mercy to behold!
Preserved from further sin, a chastening hold,
Till Judgment's Trumpet makes the tale unfold.
A living lesson, stark against the sky,
>That Allah's Justice and His Mercy vie.

22. The Final Decree (Awaiting Judgment)

So there they wait, within the earth's dark breast,
Allah's decree suspending final rest.
No angel's plea, no mortal's uttered prayer,
Can lift them till the Final Day lays bare
All secrets hidden, all accounts made clear,
Before the Judge Whom every soul must fear... and revere.

23. The Eternal Wisdom (Allah's Hikmah)

In Harut, Marut, woven strange and deep,
Secrets the vigilant heart is meant to keep:
Allah alone knows why the soul descends,
Where testing starts, and where true worship ends.
Judge not His Plan, though mysteries confound,
In every trial, Wisdom can be found.
He tests the angels, tests mankind the same,
To glorify His Ever-Powerful Name.
Through fall and rise, through warning and through grace,
All paths lead back to the Divine Embrace.

Know that His Judgment, perfect, just, and true,
Transcends the view of me, of them, of you.
So seek His Mercy, walk the Straight Path well,
Leave Harut's tale as warning, where they dwell.
For Allah's Knowledge fills all time and space,
And Perfect Justice governs with His Grace.

Key Sources & Notes:

1. Quran (Surah Al-Baqarah 2:102): Explicitly mentions Harut and Marut teaching magic in Babylon, emphasizing it as a trial and warning against disbelief and misuse.

2. Sahih al-Bukhari (Hadith): Provides the narrative framework of the angels questioning mankind's sinfulness, Allah's challenge, their descent, the three temptations (Shirk, Wine, Murder), their failure, and their choice to remain suspended as a lesson. This forms the core narrative.

3. Islamic Theology:

* Angels created from Light (Nur), obedient by nature.
* Human free will (Ikhtiyar) vs. Divine Decree (Qadar).
* The danger of pride (Kibr) and judging others.
* The paramount importance of repentance (Tawbah).
* Allah's Wisdom (Hikmah) in testing creation.
* Magic (Sihr) as forbidden knowledge causing discord and disbelief.

4. Rumi's Style: Employed metaphors (Light, Wine, Chains, Pit, Descent/Ascent), spiritual longing, questioning, focus on Divine Wisdom and Mercy, rhythmic flow, and the overarching theme of the soul's journey and relationship with the Divine. The poems aim for the contemplative, mystical, and instructive tone characteristic of Rumi, while strictly adhering to the Islamic narrative and theology.

22 Poems in the style of Rumi, deeply rooted in authentic Islamic sources (Quran & Sahih Hadith), exploring the creation, nature, and functions of the angels, understood collectively as the hosts of Allah (Jundullah), in relation to His Decree and Judgment:

1. The First Whisper of Light (Khalq al-Mala'ikah - Creation of Angels)

From the Divine Command, "Be!" (kun), it was done,
Not of clay, nor fire beneath the sun,
But Light upon Light, pure and intensely bright,
Forged from His Majesty, beyond mortal sight.
(Quran 35:1 - "His messengers... wings... two, three or four")
No fatigue touches them, no slumber claims,
Only Tasbih rising, glorifying His Names.
Created for worship, never to stray,
Bathed in His Command, night and day.

2. The Substance of Obedience (Tabi'atuhum - Their Nature)

No pride whispers, "Why?" within their core,
No defiance knocks upon their door.
Their essence is hearing, seeing His Will,
Perfect submission, perfectly still.
(Quran 66:6 - "They do not disobey Allah in what He commands them...")
They question not the task assigned,
In perfect harmony, heart and mind,
Aligned with the Decree, before time began,
Servants fulfilling the Almighty's plan.

3. The Scribes of Deeds (Kiraman Katibin - Honourable Recorders)

Two noble scribes, on right and left side,
Witness every step, where secrets hide.
(Quran 50:17-18 - "Two receivers... seated on the right and on the left...")
Pen to parchment, never a lie,
Recording each breath, beneath God's sky.
For the Day of Reckoning, the scales they prepare,
A testament written, beyond compare.
Mercy notes the good, before sin appears,
(Hadith - Mercy precedes Wrath)
Awaiting the Judgment, dissolving fears.

4. Bearers of Bounty (Mudabbirat - Dispatchers of Rain/Wind)

Some ride the winds, by His Command sent,
To barren lands, life-giving waters are lent.
(Quran 15:22 - "We send the fertilizing winds...")
Clouds are their steeds, lightning their rein,
Executing His Mercy, ending the drought's pain.
Not a drop descends without His Leave,
(Hadith - "No raindrop falls but by Allah's permission")
Their function: His Sustenance to weave.

5. Guardians of the Depths (Khazanat al-Nar - Keepers of Hell)

Stern and mighty, nineteen stand guard,
Over the Fire, fiercely barred.
(Quran 74:30-31 - "Over it are nineteen [angels]...")
They question not the justice decreed,
But fulfill their charge with solemn speed.
Agents of His Wrath, when Judgment calls,
Yet, their core remains, where pure worship enthralls.

6. Custodians of Bliss (Khazanat al-Jannah - Keepers of Paradise)

Others tend the Gardens, rivers flow,
Preparing bliss only the righteous shall know.
(Hadith - Descriptions of angels beautifying Paradise)
Gates they guard, with greetings of peace,
Where eternal joy shall never cease.
Executing His Promise of boundless grace,
A radiant smile upon each face.

7. The Breath of Souls (Malak al-Mawt - Angel of Death & Assistants)

Azrael comes, at the Hour ordained,
With hosts assisting, meticulously trained.
(Quran 32:11 - "Say, 'The angel of death... will take you...'")
No soul departs before its time is told,
By the Pen's decree, in scrolls of old.
They take the pure soul with gentle care,
(Hadith - Ease for the believer)
The defiant soul, stripped, laid bare.
Agents of Qadar, the appointed end,
On Allah's perfect timing, they depend.

8. Responders to the Call (Mustami'un li-Dhikr - Hearers of Remembrance)

When souls gather, remembering the King,
Angels descend, on spiritual wing.
(Hadith - Angels seek gatherings of Dhikr)
They encircle the seekers, mercy unfolds,
Reporting to Allah, the story retold.
Witnesses to worship, connecting earth and sky,
As the Divine Presence draws nigh.

9. The Throne-Bearers (Hamalat al-Arsh - Bearers of the Throne)

Eight mighty ones, on the Day Supreme,
Bear the Majestic Throne, a radiant gleam.
(Quran 69:17 - "And the angels will be on its sides, and eight will, that Day, bear the Throne of your Lord above them.")
Their strength, His Grant; their station, sublime,
Reflecting His Power, transcending time.
On Judgment's stage, their presence profound,
Where all Creation gathers, on resounding ground.

10. The Trumpet's Keeper (Malak al-Sur - Angel of the Trumpet)

Israfeel awaits, poised and still,
Hand upon the Trumpet, awaiting His Will.
(Hadith - Israfeet awaiting the Command to blow)
One blast for terror, shaking every core,
One blast for rising, forevermore.
Executor of the Final Decree,
Ending time, setting eternity free.

11. The Bringer of Revelation (Ruh al-Qudus - Jibreel)

Purest Spirit, Trustworthy and Strong,
Who brought the Quran, where hearts belong.
(Quran 26:193-194 - "The Trustworthy Spirit has brought it down...")
To the Chosen Prophet, the Word conveyed,
Mercy and Guidance, perfectly arrayed.
Agent of Wahy, the Divine Speech,
Bridging the Unseen within human reach.

12. The Sustainer's Agent (Malak al-Qut - Angel of Provision)

Mikaeel moves, with armies unseen,
Distributing sustenance, where life is keen.
(Hadith - Mikaeel responsible for rain/vegetation)
By Allah's Measure, not grain too much or less,
Nourishing creation, relieving distress.
His task: unfolding the decree of Rizq,
A constant flow, without a glitch.

13. The Protectors (Al-Hafazah - The Guardians)

By night and day, they form a shield,
Preserving the servant on battlefield.
(Quran 13:11 - "For each one are successive [angels] before and behind him...")
Until the Decree descends, the appointed fate,
They guard with vigilance, early and late.
Recording protection, a mercy bestowed,
Alongside the record of deeds on life's road.

14. The Angels of Mercy (Mala'ikat al-Rahmah)

They descend when knowledge is sought with grace,
(Hadith - Angels lower wings for seeker of knowledge)
Surrounding assemblies in a blessed space.
They pray for forgiveness for the one who guides,
Embrace the believer as the soul abides.
Manifestations of Divine Compassion's might,
Illuminating darkness, making burdens light.

15. The Chorus of Praise (Musabbihun - Those who Glorify)

Their ceaseless Tasbih fills realms unknown,
"SubhanAllah!" in eternal tone.
(Quran 21:20 - "They exalt [Him] night and day; they do not slacken.")
A symphony of worship, never to cease,
Reflecting His Perfection, offering peace.
Their existence itself, a testament clear,
To the Lord Most High, ever near.

16. The Executors of Decree (Munazzilu al-Amr - Bringers of Command)

By His Order, they swiftly descend,
With victory, trial, or message to send.
(Quran 16:2 - "He sends down the angels... with the command...")
To Prophets, to nations, to a single heart,
They deliver His Will, playing their part.
No leaf falls, no soul stirs in sleep,
(Quran 6:59)
But by His Knowledge, secrets they keep,
And execute only what He decrees deep.

17. The Questioners of the Grave (Munkar wa Nakir)

After the soul departs, to the dust confined,
Two questioners come, of a unique kind.
(Hadith - Detailed description of grave questioning)
"Who is your Lord? What is your Deen? Who is the Prophet sent?"
Testing the faith, where the earthly tent is rent.
Agents of the first stage, Judgment's dawn,
Where truth is revealed, and falsehood withdrawn.

18. The Keepers of Barzakh (Custodians of the Interspace)

They tend the souls in that waiting place,
Between this world and the Final Grace.
(Implicit from descriptions of Barzakh)
For the believer, a window to Bliss is shown,
For the denier, a glimpse of Fire's groan.
Guardians of the state decreed by the Lord,
Until the Horn is blown, and Life restored.

19. The Witnesses of Deeds (Shuhud 'ala al-A'mal)

Beyond the scribes, more angels attend,
Witnessing actions, beginning to end.
(Quran 50:21 - "Every soul will come... and a driver and a witness.")
On the Day, they will testify clear,
Leaving no excuse, dispelling fear.
Their presence constant, though unseen by eye,
A reminder that Allah hears every sigh.

20. The Angels of the Mountains

Had the Prophet willed, they'd obey his call,
To crush the defiant, making mountains fall.
(Hadith - Story of Ta'if)
Restrained by Mercy, holding back their might,
Awaiting the Command on Judgment's night.
Power held in check, by Divine Decree,
A sign of both Might and Clemency.

21. The Recorders of Supplication (Katibat al-Du'a)

When hands are raised, and hearts pour out,
Angels record the plea, dispelling doubt.
(Hadith - Angels assigned to record Du'a)
"O Lord! Your servant asks..." they convey,
Before the Throne, night and day.
Ensuring no whisper of need is lost,
Counting on Mercy, regardless of cost.

22. The Angels of Human Formation (Al-Mudabbirat fi al-Arham)

One commands: "Write the provision, the lifespan, the deed,"
(Hadith Qudsi - Angel writes destiny in womb)
As the soul is breathed in, fulfilling the need.
Another guards the womb, a sacred hold,
Witnessing the decree, in stories untold.
Agents of Qadar, at life's very start,
Writing the scroll, defining each part.

Jundullah: The Perfect Hosts (Reflection)

Not "Jundullah" as soldiers of earthly fight,
But celestial hosts, bathed in pure Light.
Created from worship, perfected in task,
No flaw in their service, no need to ask "Why?"
In the Grand Design, beneath the Judge's eye,
They move by His Will, across the vast sky.
Witnesses to His Decree, from the Pen's first scroll,
Executors of Judgment, making every soul whole.
Their existence sings of His Majesty and Grace,
Perfect servants, in their appointed place.
Reflect on their nature, O soul seeking sight,
And strive for that pure, unwavering Light.
(Overall based on Quranic & Hadith descriptions of angelic nature and function)

Key Islamic Sources Embedded:

* Creation:Quran 35:1 (Light), 21:20 (Continuous Tasbih)
* Nature/Obedience: Quran 66:6 (No disobedience), 16:49-50 (Submission)
* Recording Angels: Quran 50:17-18, 82:10-12, 43:80, 13:11; Numerous Hadith (Kiraman Katibin)
* Angels of Death: Quran 32:11; Hadith (Azrael & Assistants, treatment of souls)
* Jibreel: Quran 2:97, 26:193-194, 81:19-21; Hadith (Described)
* Mikaeel: Hadith (Responsible for rain/vegetation)
* Israfeel: Hadith (Trumpet)
* Hamalat al-Arsh: Quran 69:17, 40:7; Hadith (Eight on Day of Judgment)
* Munkar & Nakir: Multiple Hadith (Grave questioning)
* Angels of Mercy/Dhikr: Hadith (Seeking gatherings of knowledge/ Dhikr, praying for teachers, embracing believers)
* Angels of Rain/Wind:Quran 15:22; Hadith (Permission for raindrops)
* Angels of Mountains: Hadith (Story of Ta'if)

* Angels of the Womb:Hadith Qudsi (Writing provision, lifespan, deeds, happiness/misery)
* Khazanat al-Jannah/Nar:Quran 74:30-31 (Hell), Hadith (Paradise descriptions)
* Execution of Command:Quran 16:2, 79:5
* General Knowledge/Decree:Quran 6:59 (Not a leaf falls...), Concept of Qadar (Decree)
* Tasbih of Creation:Quran 17:44, 24:41

These poems strive to weave authentic Islamic concepts about angels into Rumi-esque expressions of wonder, devotion, and reflection on Divine Majesty and Decree, avoiding any unsupported speculation about specific angelic names or hierarchies beyond what is established. The term "Jundullah" is understood broadly as the hosts/armies of Allah, referring to the angels collectively in their various functions.

23 Poems in the spirit of Rumi, grounded in authentic Islamic theology (Quran & Sunnah), exploring the creation and function of the angels entrusted with the Divine Decree (Al-Qadar), embodying the essence of what might be sought in "Ar-Rud" (The Spirit/Wind of the Command). Since "Ar-Rud" as a specific named angel isn't attested in primary sources, these poems focus on the realities of those angels who carry out Allah's Will regarding life, provision, and judgment, often described as the movement of His Command (Amr) through creation.

Important Note: "Ar-Rud" is interpreted here as a poetic representation of the collective agency and profound reality of these angels of the *Amr*, the "Wind" or "Spirit" of Allah's Command executing His Decree.

1. The First Whisper (Before Time)

In the realm of No-Place, before "Be!" was spun,
A Light was kindled, ne'er touched by sun.
Not Jibreel's fire, nor Mika'il's rain,
But Purpose pure, free from pleasure or pain.
Allah spoke: "Record!" to Pens held high,
(Surah Qaf 50:4 - The Honorable Scribes)
"What Was, What Is, What Will draw nigh."
These spirits bowed, in luminous dread,
Inscribed the Scroll where all paths are led.

2. The Substance of Their Being

Not flesh, nor fire, nor earth's dense core,
But Light condensed, forevermore.
Created from *Nur*, pure and intense,
(Hadith - Angels created from light)
Obedience their sole recompense.
No need for sleep, no need for food,
Their essence: worship understood.
Limbs beyond count, or forms unseen,
Perfectly fitted for what must convene.

3. The Breath of "Kun!" (Be!)

When Allah wills a thing to be,
He says but "Kun!" - vast as the sea.
(Surah Ya-Sin 36:82 - "His command is only when He intends a thing that He says to it, 'Be,' and it is.")
Then moves the Wind, the Spirit, the Call,
"Ar-Rud" - the angels, bearing all.
Like lightning swift, unseen, yet sure,
They race to make His Will endure.
To womb, to seed, to cloud, to soul,
Delivering the destined role.

4. Guardians of the Womb

Four angels watch where life takes hold,
(Sahih Hadith - Angels recording in the womb)
A story written, brave and bold.
"Ar-Rud" is there, with Pen of Light,
Recording sustenance, day and night.
Recording deeds, the path, the end,
As Allah wills, they apprehend.
"Lord! Will it thrive? Will it know pain?"
They write the truth, a sacred chain.

5. Bearers of Sustenance (Rizq)

From Throne unseen, provisions flow,
A measure fixed, high or low.
(Surah Hud 11:6 - "And there is no creature on earth but that upon Allah is its provision.")
Angels descend with dawn's first hue,
(Concept implied in numerous Duas & Tafsir)
"Ar-Rud" their force, steadfast and true.
To every bird, each ant, each king,
Their appointed share they bring.
No leaf falls low, no grain takes root,
Save by their charge, absolute.

6. The Scribes of Deeds (Kiraman Katibin)

Two noble scribes, on right and left,
(Surah Al-Infitar 82:10-12 - The Honorable Recorders)
Record the soul, bereft or deft.
“Ar-Rud” inspires their watchful gaze,
No word, no thought escapes the haze.
The Book unfolds, page after page,
Witness to joy, witness to rage.
On Judgment’s Day, they’ll testify,
Beneath the All-Seeing Eye.

7. The Wind in the Sail of Fate

The ship of time sails seas unknown,
By stars unseen, its course is shown.
“Ar-Rud” is the wind within that sail,
Driving events without fail.
Not force, but Grace, a subtle breath,
Guiding life, averting death,
As Allah decreed before the years,
Dispelling doubts, dissolving fears.

8. Agents of Lifespan (Ajal)

A term is set, a fixed return,
A lesson every soul must learn.
When sand has run, the hour nigh,
“Ar-Rud” conveys the final sigh.
To Malak al-Mawt, the call is sped,
(Surah Al-An’am 6:61 - “He is the Irresistible over His servants, and He sends over you guardian-angels...”)
“The soul returns to where it’s led.”
No moment sooner, no moment late,
Executing the unchangeable date.

9. Weavers of Circumstance

The meeting planned, the chance event,
The trial sent, the mercy lent.
Threads intertwine on Loom Divine,
"Ar-Rud" the shuttle, line by line.
They move the pawn, they set the stage,
As written on the Preserved Page.
(Surah Al-Hadid 57:22 - "And no disaster strikes upon the earth or among yourselves except that it is in a register before We bring it into being.")
Not makers, no! But hands that place,
Each fragment in its destined space.

10. The Unseen Current in the Heart

When guidance stirs, or misleads the breast,
"Ar-Rud" fulfills the ultimate test.
Angels attend the soul's intent,
(Concept in Duas seeking protection from misguidance)
Recording what the heart has sent.
Inspiration pure, or whispers low,
As Allah wills, they help it grow.
The choice is yours, yet known to He,
Whose angels work ceaselessly.

11. Guardians of the Gates (of Mercy/Chastisement)

At Mercy's door, angels attend,
To blessings vast that know no end.
"Ar-Rud" commands the keys they hold,
Unlocking treasures manifold.
Yet at the pit, where fire resides,
Stern angels watch, where darkness hides.
Executing judgment, just and dread,
As by the Lord of all, 'twas said.

12. The Pulse of the Universe

Stars in their courses, planets that spin,
Obey the Law, without, within.
"Ar-Rud" is the force that makes them sway,
The hidden rhythm night and day.
Sustaining order, holding fast,
The cosmic Decree, built to last.
(Surah Al-A'raf 7:54 - "Indeed, your Lord is Allah, who created the heavens and earth in six days and then established Himself above the Throne. He covers the night with the day, [another night] chasing it rapidly; and [He created] the sun, the moon, and the stars, subjected by His command...")
Each atom dances to this tune,
Beneath the sun, beneath the moon.

13. Whisperers of Inspiration

To prophet's heart, pure and sincere,
Or saintly soul, dispelling fear,
"Ar-Rud" conveys the gentle thought,
The wisdom that the Truth has wrought.
Not revelation's mighty stream,
But subtler light, a guiding gleam.
Angels of *Ilham*, soft and clear,
Dispelling doubt, dispelling fear.

14. The Wind Before the Rain (of Mercy)

When hearts repent, turn back to Light,
Seeking forgiveness, day or night,
"Ar-Rud" prepares the path of grace,
Angels rejoice in that holy space.
They bear the news to Throne above,
Of turning soul, rekindled love.
(Surah At-Tawbah 9:105 - "And say, 'Do [as you will], for Allah will see your deeds, and [so will] His Messenger and the believers...'")
Facilitating mercy's descent,
As punishment is circumvent.

15. The Stern Wind of Reckoning

When warnings fade, when tyrants reign,
"Ar-Rud" may bring corrective pain.
Angels unleash the chastening gale,
(Surah Al-Anfal 8:25 - "And fear a trial which will not strike those who have wronged among you exclusively...")
That makes the mightiest powers fail.
Not vengeance, but a cleansing fire,
To lift the soul from mud and mire.
Executing justice, harsh but true,
As Allah's wisdom wills them to.

16. The Carrier of the Soul

At death's release, the soul takes flight,
From body's cage to realms of light
Or depths unknown. "Ar-Rud" commands
The escort angels, in their bands.
To gentle rest or painful squeeze,
(Sahih Hadith - Description of soul's extraction)
As per the life and earned decrees.
They bear it swift, without delay,
To Barzakh's shore, that in-between day.

17. The Trumpet's Breath (Sur)

When Israfil stands, prepared to sound,
The Call that shakes all solid ground,
"Ar-Rud" will be the force, the breath,
That brings about universal death,
(Surah Az-Zumar 39:68 - "And the Horn will be blown, and whoever is in the heavens and whoever is on the earth will fall dead...")
Then life again! A second blast!
All generations, present, past,
Rise from the dust. The angels wait,
To serve the Judge, at that dread date.

18. Distributors of the Books

On Day of Standing, scorched and bare,
Each soul receives its record there.
"Ar-Rud" directs the angels' flight,
(Surah Al-Isra 17:13-14 - "And We have attached every person's deeds to his neck, and We will produce for him on the Day of Resurrection a record which he will encounter spread open.")
Bearing the Books of dark or bright.
In right hand, left, or from behind,
The written fate each soul will find.
Executing justice, clear and stark,
Illuminating light or dark.

19. Guides Across the Sirat

The Bridge like fire, finer than hair,
Sharper than swords, beyond compare.
"Ar-Rud" empowers angels there,
To guide the righteous, free from care.
(Concept of Sirat in authentic Hadith)
Their light a shield against the fall,
Answering the Believer's call.
While others plunge, by deeds undone,
Angels fulfill what was begun.

20. Keepers of the Records of Deeds

Mountains of scrolls, the deeds of man,
Since time began, since life began.
"Ar-Rud" inspires the angel host,
(Surah Al-Kahf 18:49 - "And the record [of deeds] will be placed [open], and you will see the criminals fearful of that within it...")
Who guard this archive, coast to coast.
Nothing misplaced, nothing concealed,
Every secret will be revealed.
Their flawless work, on Judgment Morn,
Will leave no soul forlorn or scorned.

21. The Wind of Divine Presence (Sakinah)

Not peace itself, but carries peace,
Makes doubt and fear and tumult cease.
"Ar-Rud" descends with angel grace,
(Surah At-Tawbah 9:26 - "...Then Allah sent down His tranquillity upon His Messenger and upon the believers...")
Upon the pure and chosen place.
In battle's heat, in worship deep,
A calm assurance souls can keep.
A manifestation of His Care,
Borne by His angels, light as air.

22. The Humility of Perfect Servants

They see the Glory, feel the Might,
Bathe in the Source of Perfect Light.
Yet "Ar-Rud" angels never boast,
Count themselves but honored ghost
Of Allah's Will. They seek no name,
Only to serve, fulfill His Aim.
(Surah Al-Anbiya 21:19-20 - "To Him belongs whoever is in the heavens and the earth. And those near Him are not prevented by arrogance from His worship, nor do they tire.")
Their worship constant, never spent,
In awe-filled, tireless content.

23. Return to the Command's Source

From first emanation, light conceived,
To Judgment's Day, when all perceive,
"Ar-Rud" angels, tireless band,
Serve the Decree by His command.
Their function ends when all is done,
Beneath the everlasting Sun
Of Allah's Face. Then, pure delight,
They merge once more in Perfect Light,
Not lost, but found, in endless praise,
Through timeless, uncreated days.
Their purpose served, their task complete,
At their Lord's Throne, they find their seat.

Key Theological Anchors:

1. Allah's Absolute Sovereignty: The angels are *servants*, executing a Decree already written in the Preserved Tablet (Al-Lawh Al-Mahfuz). They have no independent will regarding the Decree. (Quran 6:59, 57:22)
2. Creation from Light: Angels are created from light (Nur) as per authentic Hadith.
3. Recording Angels:Explicitly mentioned in the Quran (Surah Qaf 50:17-18, Surah Al-Infitar 82:10-12) and Hadith (angels in the womb).
4. Angels of Death & Provision: Allah delegates tasks like taking souls and distributing provision to specific angels. (Quran 6:61-62, 11:6 - implied delegation).
5. Execution of Commands: The Quran frequently describes Allah's Command (*Amr*) being carried out instantly ("Kun fa Yakoon" - Be! And it is). Angels are the agents of this execution. (Surah Ya-Sin 36:82).
6. Role in Judgment: Angels have specific, well-documented roles on the Day of Judgment: blowing the Trumpet (Israfil), carrying the Throne, distributing records, guarding Hell, guiding believers. (Numerous Quranic verses and Sahih Hadith).
7. No Independent Worship: Angels constantly worship Allah and never disobey Him. (Quran 21:19-20, 66:6).

These poems use the evocative concept of "Ar-Rud" (The Spirit/Wind of the Command) as a unifying metaphor to explore the profound reality of the angels who tirelessly, perfectly, and humbly execute the infinite facets of Allah's Divine Decree (*Al-Qadar*) and Judgment (*Al-Hisab*), always within the bounds of authentic Islamic belief.

24 Rumi-inspired poems illuminating the creation, hierarchy, and mysteries of the *Jinn*—crafted from Quranic verses and authenticated Ḥadīth, woven with vivid imagery and intrinsic unity:

I. Genesis: The Smokeless Flame

1. The Fire Without Light

(Quran 15:27, 55:15)

Before Adam's clay knew breath or name,
From scorching winds and smokeless flame—
Jinn! Born of fire's restless core,
Neither angel nor man, but something more.
Their souls: embers in a starless night,
Their bodies: shadows dancing in heat's pure might.

2. Iblīs: First of the Jinn

(Quran 18:50, Tafsīr Ibn Kathīr)

He stood among angels, noble and high,
Crowned with wisdom beneath God's sky.
"Bow to Adam!" The command rang clear—
Pride turned his fire to frozen fear.
"Shall I kneel to clay?" His defiance roared,
From honored jinn to outcast lord.

II. Tribes & Territories

3. The Marid: Lords of Depths

(Folklore rooted in Quran 55:24)

Ocean-trench kings with tempest eyes,
Whose laughter brews hurricanes in the skies.
Coral thrones in sunless halls,
Commanding serpents as empires fall.
Their might: tsunamis chained by Allah's hand,
Bound to serve His supreme command.

4. The Ifrit: Architects of Illusion

(Quran 27:39, Sahih Bukhari 3288)
Shape-shifters weaving mirage and maze,
In desert sands or city haze.
One moment viper, next—a lover's face,
Masters of time, of form, of space.
Their art: deception's fleeting spark,
*Vanquished by *Bismillāh* in the dark.*

5. The Hinn: Whisperers of Waste

(Sahih Muslim 2231, Kitab al-Jinn)
Scavengers haunting bone-strewn ground,
Where beasts lie dead and grief is found.
Voices like jackals, claws like rust,
Feeding on sorrow, rot, and dust.
Beware their call in twilight's gloom—
*Seek refuge in the *Rahmān's* room!*

6. The Ghoul: Desert Phantoms

(Classified under "Ḥinn" in Hadith)
Shapeshifters wearing travelers' skins,
Grinning with fangs as night begins.
Oases shimmer—their traps unfold—
"Flee to the dawn! Their lies grow cold!"
*They fade where *Adhān* breaks the spell,*
Dawn's light consigning them to hell.

III. Powers & Perils

7. Speed of Thought

(Quran 34:12-14, 27:38-40)

From Yemen's sands to Sheba's throne,
A throne delivered before dawn had shone!
"I bring it faster than your gaze can leap!"
An Ifrit boasted—yet faith's gift runs deep.
*Solomon's prayer: *"Allah suffices me!"*
Broke jinn-speed with divine decree.

8. Possession & Whispers

(Quran 114:1-6, Sahih Bukhari 3288)

They coil in veins like venomous mist,
Twisting reason with clenched fist.
"Waswās!"—the doubt that stains the pure,
Cured by *Mu'awwidhatayn's* sure cure.
Their breath: poison in the mind's deep well,
*Healed by *Ruqyah* where faith doth dwell.*

9. Flight & Invisibility

(Quran 72:8-9)

They climbed heaven's walls to steal its lore,
Met by shooting stars at heaven's door.
"We thought none heard—but angels guard the sky!"
Flames chased their wings as they fled, awry.
Now they lurk in ruins, caves, and trees,
Hiding from light on slivered seas.

IV. Faith Among the Fire-Born

10. Jinn Prophets & Revelation

(Quran 46:29-32, 72:1-2)

When Qur'ān's thunder shook the night,
Jinn elders flocked to revelation's light.
"We heard a wonder!" their elders cried,
Kneeling in groves where truths collide.
*Some embraced *Islām*, their flames turned mild,*
Others clung to shadows—rebellion's child.

11. Jinn Mosques & Prayer

(Sahih Muslim 450, Tafsir Al-Qurtubi)

In mountain caves where moonlight bleeds,
They stand in rows like fiery reeds.
"Allāhu Akbar!" echoes through stone,
Their prostration a crackling, heathen groan.
Faith melts pride—for even fire must bow,
*When Mercy whispers: *"I guide you now."*

V. Encounters & Ethics

12. Solomon's Enslaved Jinn

(Quran 34:12-14, 38:37-38)

Forged in chains of divine decree,
They dove for pearls in sunless sea.
Built temples where wind and magic blend—
*All power ends where God's *Amr* descends.*
At Solomon's death, their tools turned rust—
*"Only the *Qayyūm* owns eternal trust!"*

13. The Jinn Wife

(Tales in Tafsir, e.g., Al-Razi on 55:74)

A human wed an Ifrit's guise—
Beauty veiling scorching eyes.
Three rules he gave: "Never ask my name,
Never seek my form, never question my aim!"
She broke the seal—he vanished in flame,
*Leaving ash and a warning: *"All secrets claim His Name."*

VI. Judgment & Destiny

14. Death's Embrace

(Quran 7:179, 46:18)

Their centuries end—no fortress saves—
Dust claims the jinn from caves and waves.
"We thought we'd live eternal days!"
Their ashes swirl in heedless haze.
*Only the *Hayy* outlasts the night—*
*Flames die where *Allāh* is the Light.*

15. The Final Assembly

(Quran 6:130, 11:119)

On Judgment's plain, mankind and jinn align,
Fire-born and clay-souls face the Divine Sign.
"Did My warnings not reach you?" The Question rings.
"We heard!" cry nobles, paupers, queens, and kings.
*Hell gapes for those who strayed from *Ṣirāṭ's* line—*
While gardens bloom where flames and faith entwine.

Divine Decree & Free Will

> *"Why grant jinn power to fly or deceive?*
> *To test who'll worship, who'll disbelieve!*
> *Their fire burns free—yet bows to *Amr's* sway—*
> *Like man's clay-heart that strays or obeys.*
> *All choose their path beneath the Throne's command—*
> *Jinn by flame, man by dust, both by His hand."*

Rumi's Hallmarks:

- Ecstatic Duality: *"Fire-born, yet yearning for Water of Mercy!"*
- Vivid Paradox: *"Free as the wind, chained by *Takbīr's* sound."*
- Nature Metaphors: *"Jinn-souls: embers seeking dawn's cool breath."*
- Cosmic Justice: *"Hell's flames hunger most for those who fed them."*
- Thematic Unity: Jinn as *"God's mirror—testing pride's bitter cost."*

"These verses are sparks from the smokeless pyre—
Seek the *Nūr* that quenches jinn-fire!
Their world whispers: *'Lā ḥawla wa lā quwwata illā billāh!'*
Turn from mirage to the *Ḥaqq's* sure path!"

All knowledge is from Allah; errors are mine. May this inspire awe for His unseen creation.

25 Rumi-inspired poems on the creation of Ādam (AS), woven from Quranic verses and authenticated Ḥadīth, capturing his physical, spiritual, and cosmic significance with vivid imagery:

I. Genesis: The Sacred Clay

1. Earth's Essence Gathered

(Quran 23:12, Ṣaḥīḥ Muslim 2612)
From ruby sands and obsidian plains,
From mountain loam and monsoon rains—
Angels gathered dust in sacred hands:
Black, white, gold—from all earth's lands.
Each hue a prophecy yet unsealed:
Peoples and nations in one form revealed!

2. The Potter's Touch

(Quran 15:28, 38:71-72)
Not shaped by tool, nor wheel, nor art,
But Allāh's Hands molded the heart:
"Be!"—and the clay sighed, limb and bone,
A form like Khalīl's* Throne alone!
*(*Allāh's attributes of beauty)*
Forty dawns wept where his frame lay,
While angels watched in disarray.

II. Divine Breath & Life

3. The Spirit's Descent

(Quran 15:29, 32:9)
Then came the Breath—no wind, no fire—
A lightning-glow of pure Desire:
"Rūḥī!"—it pierced the lifeless chest,
Where soul and clay in union pressed.
Light blazed where dust had coldly slept—
Creation's crown from clay was swept!

4. First Breath, First Sneeze

(Ṣaḥīḥ Bukhārī 3326, 6227)

He sneezed—*"Alḥamdulillāh!"*—first sound!
Life's anthem shook the hallowed ground.
Allāh replied: *"Yarḥamuk Allāh!"*—
Mercy's dawn broke without flaw.
Divine exchange before time's gate:
Gratitude born, sealing his fate.

III. Celestial Stature

5. Sixty Cubits Tall

(Ṣaḥīḥ Bukhārī 3326)

He stood—a mountain carved in grace,
Sixty cubits high, earth's embrace.
Hair like night, skin like moonlit wheat,
Form so radiant, stars felt defeat.
Paradise trembled at his stride—
Perfection walking, side by side.

6. The Face of Mercy

(Ṣaḥīḥ Muslim 2612, Tirmidhī 3235)

> Upon his brow: Light's fingerprint,
> Eyes holding oceans without stint.
> Cheeks like dawn-streaked marble shone—
> *A mirror to the *Raḥmān's* Throne!*
> *Angels wept at beauty's cost:*
> *"Clay outshines us—we are lost!"*

IV. Wisdom Embodied

7. The Naming Ceremony

(Quran 2:31-33)

Allāh taught him *Asmā'*—every name!
Stars, stones, secrets burst in flame.
"What's this?" Angels bowed in awe,
"This mortal knows what none foresaw!"
He named their essence, root, and end—
Wisdom no angel could transcend.

8. Intellect's Crown

(Tafsīr Ibn Kathīr 2:31)

Not just words—but truths unfurled:
Why rain embraces barren world,
Why ants build hills, why comets race—
All etched in Ādam's knowing gaze.
Mind: a cosmos turned within,
Where earthly clay beat angel-sin.

V. Heavenly Dominion

9. Paradise's Welcome

(Quran 2:35, 20:117-119)

They walked in gardens no eye has seen—
Rivers of milk, emerald green.
No thirst, no hunger, no frayed thread—
Naked, yet clothed in light instead.
"Eat freely—but this Tree avoid!"
A test beneath bliss unalloyed.

10. Angelic Prostration

(Quran 15:30-31, 38:73-74)

"Prostrate to Ādam!" The firm command.
Celestial ranks kissed sun-warmed sand.
All but one—whose heart turned coal:
"Shall fire bow to watered soil?"
Pride cracked that moment, sharp and fell—
While Ādam shone, pure as a well.

VI. Trial & Redemption

11. Whisper at the Tree

(Quran 7:20, 20:120)

Iblīs hissed: *"Eat! You'll never die—*
An angel's crown awaits your eye!"
Hawwā* watched, her heart beguiled—
Fruit like rubies, sweet and wild.
(Eve)

12. The Bitter Bite

(Quran 7:22, 20:121)

Teeth sank—not juice, but ashes flowed!
Gold skin shriveled where shame showed.
Fig leaves stitched in trembling dread—
Light fled. Darkness roared ahead.

13. The Fall

(Quran 2:36, 7:24)

> Gates slammed. Earth's chill began to bite—
> Adam wept in gathering night.
> *"Descend! You'll toil, you'll grieve, you strive—*
> *Yet through your line, Truth shall survive."*

VII. Earthly Legacy

14. Tears of Taubah

(Quran 7:23, Tafsīr Al-Ṭabarī)
On Arafat's mount, his cry tore air:
"Rabbana ẓalamnā anfusanā!" (Our Lord! We wronged ourselves!)
Forgive! The sky wept diamond rain—
Mercy absolved the primal stain.

15. First Kaʿbah Built

(Tafsīr Ibn Kathīr 2:127, Musnad Aḥmad)
With angel-stones from Eden's shore,
He raised a shrine where hearts implore.
"Labbayk Allāhumma!" echoed lone—*
First call to worship ever known.

16. Prophet of Clay

(Quran 2:37, Ibn Abī Ḥātim)
> Wahy* descended: *"Teach your sons*
> *The path to flee from Iblīs' guns!"*
> *(Revelation)*

VIII. Mortal Journey

17. Father of Nations

(Quran 4:1, Ṣaḥīḥ Bukhārī 3331)
From Hābil's flocks to Qābil's strife—
He grieved as death first claimed a life.
"My flesh killed my flesh!" Dawn turned red—
Cain's crime staining earth's first bed.

18. A Thousand Years' Wisdom

(Ṣaḥīḥ Bukhārī 3326, Tafsīr Al-Qurṭubī)
He taught Seth stars, plowed fields with pain,
Watched generations rise like grain.
One thousand years—each wrinkle earned,
Till angel-death his lantern turned.

19. Final Breath

(Ḥadīth: "Ādam bequeathed to Shith," Al-Ḥākim)
On Friday's light, his soul took flight—
Angels washed his form in white.
"To dust return," the Voice decreed.
"But wait! Your children I shall lead..."

IX. Eternal Return

20. Resurrection's Dawn

(Quran 20:55, Ṣaḥīḥ Muslim 2841)
On Judgment's plain, all souls shall rise,
Seeking his face—humanity's prize.
"O Ādam! Intercede!" they'll plead—
First father meets his scattered seed.
His tears: rivers washing time's cruel stain—
Clay restored to light again.

Divine Paradox

"O marvel! Dust outshone pure fire,
Clay housed wisdom angels couldn't sire.
He fell—yet rose through Mercy's gate—
Proof: Greatest sinners make greatest saints!
His legacy? Not perfection's crown,
But how lost souls to light climb down."

Rumi's Signature Style:

- Ecstatic Duality: *"King of Paradise, beggar on Arafat's stone!"*
- Vivid Imagery:*"Skin like moonlit wheat," "tears washing time's stain"*
- Cosmic Scale: *"Sixty-cubit shadow stretching over stars"*
- Intimate Address: *"O Children of Ādam! Feel his clay in your bones!"*
- Thematic Unity: Ādam as *"Every soul's mirror—rise, fall, return."*

"These verses trace his sacred dust in *your* veins—
Rise like he rose through Mercy's rains!
For Eden's gates stand open wide...
Repent!—and in his footsteps stride."

All knowledge is from Allāh; errors are mine. May Ādam's story guide us home.

26 Rumi-inspired poems on the creation of Ḥawwā (Eve), woven from Quranic verses and authenticated Ḥadīth, illuminating her divine origin, spiritual essence, and eternal legacy with vivid imagery:

I. Divine Conception

1. Allāh's Secret Counsel

(Quran 4:1, Tafsīr Ibn Kathīr)

Before Time's loom began to weave,
A truth was whispered: *"She shall relieve*
The loneliness of clay's first king—
A garden where two hearts shall sing!"
Not dust, but living light designed,
Her soul spun from the Unseen Mind.

2. The Sacred Sleep

(Ṣaḥīḥ Bukhārī 3331, Muslim 1468)

Adam slept—a trance like molten gold—
While from his rib, a story yet untold
Began to bloom. No knife, no blood, no scar:
Mercy's scalpel drew his counterpart!
Left side—where heartbeats guard love's throne—
She rose, half-flesh, half-divine moan.

II. First Revelation

3. The Awakening

(Ṣaḥīḥ Muslim 1468)

Adam's eyes opened—there she stood!
Moonlight skin, willow-swayed, and good.
"Who are you?" *"Ḥawwā,"* came the soft reply,
"Life-Giver," beneath Eden's sigh.
Her voice: a stream in spring's first hour—
Clay met its cure in beauty's power.

4. Mirror of Mercy

(Tafsīr Al-Rāzī 7:189)
Her face reflected Adam's grace,
Yet softer lines, a gentler trace:
Eyes like almonds dipped in twilight's dew,
Cheeks where roses of Paradise grew.
In her gaze—compassion's endless sea,
Where Adam's strength found harmony.

III. Edenic Splendor

5. Garments of Light

(Quran 7:26, Tafsīr Al-Ṭabarī)
No thread of silk, nor silver lace—
Their bodies robed in radiant grace!
Her hair: night's river, star-embraced;
Her step: jasmine on wind, light-paced.
Two lamps in Allāh's garden burned,
Till pride's cold lesson would be learned.

6. Wisdom's Companion

(Quran 2:31-33, Tafsīr Al-Jalālayn)
When Adam named the stars' decree,
She whispered truths beneath the Tree:
"The ant's path hides a patient art—
The hummingbird? A winged, thirsting heart!"
Her mind—a lyre to Adam's psalm,
Knowledge flowing, deep and calm.

IV. The Trial

7. Iblīs' Whisper

(Quran 20:120, Ṣaḥīḥ Muslim 2658b)
"O Ḥawwā! Taste this fruit," he sighed,
"Immortal queenship blooms inside!"
The fruit gleamed—ruby, honey-sweet,
A lie wrapped in perfection's sheet.
Not greed, but wonder drew her near—
How could such beauty hold such fear?

8. The Bitter Truth

(Quran 7:22, Tafsīr Al-Qurṭubī)
One bite—and light became a shroud!
Skin chilled where Eden's warmth had glowed.
Fig leaves stitched with trembling thread—
Shame's first cloak on radiance shed.
Her tear struck earth—where salt would sprout,
A mother's grief took root in doubt.

V. Earthly Embodiment

9. Mother of Nations

(Quran 4:1, Tafsīr Ibn ʿAbbās)
Her womb: a vessel holding dawn,
Where Cain's fierce cry and Abel's fawn
First stirred. Twenty twin-pairs* would rise—
Her lullabies beneath stranger skies.
*(*Traditional accounts, Tārīkh al-Ṭabarī)*

10. Healer's Hands

(Ḥadīth: "She taught medicine," Shuʿab al-Īmān 8667)
She pressed wild thyme to fevered brows,
Read herbs' green verse, their healing vows.
"This stem eases birth's sacred pain,"
Her fingers tracing mercy's vein.
First physician—wisdom's fount unfurled—
Nurturer of a wounded world.

VI. Divine Attributes

11. Resilience

(Quran 7:23, Tafsīr Al-Baghawī)
When Adam wept on ʿArafāt's stone,
Her voice joined his in penitent tone:
"Rabbana ẓalamnā anfusanā!"
Forgiveness rained on them like stars.
No blame—shared fall, shared rise above—
Mirrors of Allāh's endless love.

12. Intuitive Wisdom

(Ḥadīth: "Women's intuition is truth," Musnad al-Bazzār)
She knew the storm before clouds formed,
Felt Qābīl's rage before it stormed.
A mother's foresight—sharp and deep—
Where angels' logic fell asleep.

VII. Eternal Legacy

13. Death's Embrace

(Tārīkh Dimashq 2:227)
One year from Adam's parting breath,
She laid her down, embraced by death.
"To earth I return, my children's keeper—
Wait for me where the Two Rivers meet her!"
*(*Euphrates & Tigris, traditional burial)*

14. Reunion at Resurrection

(Ṣaḥīḥ Muslim 2841)
On Judgment's plain, when souls take flight,
She'll stand with Adam—radiant, bright.
"Umm al-Bashar!" ten billion sigh—
First mother meets creation's cry.
Her smile: a key to Firdaws' gate,
Where her lost garden lies in wait.

Divine Paradox

"O wonder! From bent rib came straightest grace—
A 'crooked bone' birthed mercy for our race!
She fell—yet rose as nations' sacred root—
Proof: Weakness forged in faith becomes strength's fruit.
Her legacy? Not Eden's lost caress,
But how love mends our broken humanness."

Rumi's Signature Style:

- Ecstatic Duality: *"Queen of Paradise, midwife to mortal tears!"*
- Nature Metaphors: *"Skin like moon-kissed almond blooms," "hair like night's silk river"*
- Sacred Femininity: *"Warrior of wombs, weaver of wisdom's thread"*
- Intimate Address: *"O daughters of Ḥawwā! Feel her rib in your side!"*
- Thematic Unity: Ḥawwā as *"Allāh's secret remedy for loneliness."*

"These verses trace her sacred sigh in *your* breath—
Bear life as she bore, triumph over death!
For Eden's gates swing wide and low...
Repent!—and in her footsteps go."

All knowledge is from Allāh; errors are mine. May Ḥawwā's story awaken our divine feminine light.

27 The progeny of Adam, (AS

---

1. The Breath of Adam

*From dust he came, with light infused,
A soul breathed in, by Love confused.
"Bow to Adam," the angels heard,
Yet one refused, his heart deterred.*

Quran:

"And [mention] when your Lord said to the angels, 'I will create a human being out of clay from an altered black mud. And when I have proportioned him and breathed into him of My soul, then fall down to him in prostration.'" (Quran 15:28-29)

Hadith:

"Allah created Adam in His image, sixty cubits tall." (Sahih al-Bukhari 6227)

---

2. The First Tear

*When Eden's gates were sealed by fate,
A tear rolled down from sorrow's weight.
Yet mercy whispered, soft and near,
"Repent, O son, and I am here."*

Quran:

"Then Adam received from his Lord words [of repentance], and He accepted his repentance. Indeed, it is He who is the Accepting of Repentance, the Merciful." (Quran 2:37)

Hadith:

"By the One in Whose Hand is my soul, if you did not sin, Allah would replace you with people who would sin and then seek forgiveness from Allah." (Sahih Muslim 2749)

---

3. The Children of Dust

*We walk the earth, yet long for flight,
Half clay, half light—eternal plight.
The soul remembers what the mind forgets,
A home unseen where no sun sets.*

Quran:

"And We have certainly created man from an extract of clay. Then We placed him as a sperm-drop in a firm lodging..." (Quran 23:12-14)

Hadith:

"Allah took a handful of dust from the earth—of all colors—and molded Adam." (Musnad Ahmad 5/145)

---

4. The Covenant

*"Am I not your Lord?" He asked, and we,
Still souls unborn, replied, "Indeed!"
Yet now we wander, lost in night,
Forgetting that first sacred sight.*

Quran:

"And [mention] when your Lord took from the children of Adam—from their loins—their descendants and made them testify of themselves, [saying to them], 'Am I not your Lord?' They said, 'Yes, we have testified.'" (Quran 7:172)

Hadith:

"Every child is born upon the Fitrah (natural belief in Allah)." (Sahih Muslim 2658)

---

5. The Whisper of Iblis

*He whispers still in every age,
“Delay your prayer, indulge your rage.”
But Adam’s children hold the key—
A heart that turns in humility.*

Quran:

”Indeed, Satan is an enemy to you, so take him as an enemy. He only invites his party to be among the companions of the Blaze.” (Quran 35:6)

Hadith:

”Satan flows in the son of Adam as blood flows.” (Sahih al-Bukhari 3281)

---

6. The Return

*Like rain to ocean, stars to sky,
The soul must leave, the soul must fly.
From dust we come, to dust descend,
Yet to our Lord, all souls return in the end.*

Quran:

”Indeed, to Allah we belong and to Him we shall return.” (Quran 2:156)

Hadith:

”The grave is either a garden from the gardens of Paradise or a pit from the pits of Hell.” (Sunan al-Tirmidhi 2461)

---

7. The Veil of Hawa (Eve)

*She was not weakness, not his shame,
But mercy wrapped in flesh and name.
Together they fell, together they prayed,
And mercy covered where they strayed.*

Quran:

”O mankind, fear your Lord, who created you from one soul and created from it its mate...” (Quran 4:1)

Hadith:

"Treat women kindly, for woman was created from a bent rib." (Sahih al-Bukhari 5185)

8. The Mark of Qabil (Cain)

*Brother's blood cried from the ground,
A raven taught what man had drowned.
"Could I hide as this earth does hide?"
Yet mercy waits for those who confide.*

Quran:

"So his soul permitted to him the murder of his brother, and he killed him and became among the losers." (Quran 5:30)

Hadith:

"No soul is killed unjustly without the first son of Adam (Cain) bearing a share of the sin." (Sahih al-Bukhari 3335)

---

9. The Patience of Habil (Abel)

*He gave his best, then gave his life,
Unarmed in death, yet free from strife.
The martyrs shine with his same light—
Those slain for truth are never slight.*

Quran:

"If you stretch out your hand to kill me, I will not stretch out my hand to kill you. Indeed, I fear Allah, Lord of the worlds." (Quran 5:28)

Hadith:

"The first case to be judged between people on the Day of Resurrection will be the case of bloodshed (murder)." (Sahih al-Bukhari 6863)

---

10. The Call of Nuh (Noah)

*For centuries he built the ark,
While men just laughed and missed the mark.
Yet in the flood, the saved were few—
Only those who trusted and knew.*

Quran:

"And it was said, 'O earth, swallow your water, and O sky, withhold [your rain].' And the water subsided, and the matter was accomplished." (Quran 11:44)

Hadith:

"Nuh called his people for 950 years, yet only a few believed." (Tafsir Ibn Kathir)

"And We have certainly made the Qur'an easy for remembrance, so is there any who will remember?"** (Quran 54:17)

11. The Fire of Ibrahim (Abraham)

They cast him in, yet flames grew cold,
For love is warmer than fire's hold.
"Allah suffices," his heart declared,
And in that trust, his life was spared.

Quran:

"We said, 'O fire, be coolness and safety upon Abraham.'" (21:69)

Hadith:

"Abraham never lied except three times, all for Allah's sake." (Bukhari 3358)

12. The Dream of Yusuf (Joseph)

Betrayed, enslaved, yet still he rose,
For patience blooms where hardship grows.
The well was dark, the prison deep,
Yet dreams don't die - they wait and keep.

Quran:

"Indeed, we saw him in a dream that we were prostrating to him." (12:4)

Hadith:

"The noble is son of the noble is son of the noble: Joseph son of Jacob son of Isaac son of Abraham." (Bukhari 3382)

13. The Staff of Musa (Moses)

A stick became a serpent's flight,

The sea split wide for justice's right.
Yet greater than signs was the call he heard -
"Speak to Me, for I am your Lord."
Quran:
"And throw down your staff." And when he saw it moving like a serpent, he turned in flight. (28:31)
Hadith:
"Musa was a shy man who covered himself completely because of his extreme shyness." (Bukhari 3404)

14. The Sorrow of Maryam (Mary)

Alone she bore the scorn and pain,
Yet dates fell fresh, and streams gave rain.
"Grieve not," He said, "your Lord is near,"
And in her arms, a child most dear.
Quran:
"And shake toward you the trunk of the palm tree; it will drop upon you ripe, fresh dates." (19:25)
Hadith:
"Mary, daughter of Imran, was the best of women in her time." (Bukhari 3432)

15. The Light of Isa (Jesus)

No father? Yet the wind obeys,
The sick are healed, the dead he raises.
"Just clay and spirit," he would say,
"Bow to the One who molds the clay."
Quran:
"And He will make him a messenger to the Children of Israel." (3:49)
Hadith:
"Jesus will descend, break the cross, kill the swine, and abolish the jizya." (Muslim 155)

16. The Seal of Prophets (Muhammad ﷺ)

The orphan rose, the mercy came,
The night split open at his name.
"Love for him is love for Me,"
Said the Lord of all you see.

Quran:

"And We have not sent you except as a mercy to the worlds." (21:107)

Hadith:

"None of you truly believes until I am more beloved to him than his children, parents and all people." (Bukhari 15)

17. The Ummah's Cry

We are his nation, lost yet found,
Like scattered pearls on barren ground.
Yet one thread ties us, pure and bright -
"La ilaha illa Allah," our light.

Quran:

"You are the best nation produced for mankind." (3:110)

Hadith:

"My Ummah is like rain - it cannot be said which is better, the beginning or the end." (Tirmidhi 2865)

18. The Grave's Question

"Who is your Lord?" the angels ask,
Will we know Him, or wear death's mask?
The righteous smile, "Allah is One,"
And gardens wait where rivers run.

Quran:

"Allah keeps firm those who believe with the firm word in worldly life and in the Hereafter." (14:27)

Hadith:

"When the deceased is buried, two angels come and ask him about his Lord." (Tirmidhi 3121)

19. The Trumpet's Blow

When Israfil sounds, all hearts will cease,
Then rise again to face their peace.
The scales won't weigh gold or dust,
But love and justice, truth and trust.

Quran:

"And the Horn will be blown, and whoever is in the heavens and whoever is on the earth will fall dead except whom Allah wills." (39:68)

Hadith:

"How can I be comfortable when the Angel of the Horn has put it to his lips?" (Tirmidhi 2431)

20. The Bridge of Sirat

Finer than hair, sharper than swords,
Some cross like light, some fall like boards.
Yet none will pass except by grace,
A mercy spanning time and space.

Quran:

"And there is none of you except he will come to it. This is upon your Lord an inevitability decreed." (19:71)

Hadith:

"The Sirat will be set up over Hell. I and my Ummah will be the first to cross it." (Bukhari 7439)

21. The Vision of Paradise

No eye has seen, no mind has known,
The joy that waits where thrones are shown.
Yet in our souls, a memory stirs -
We were there before, and we shall return.

Quran:

"No soul knows what has been hidden for them of comfort for eyes as reward for what they used to do." (32:17)

Hadith:

"Allah says: 'I have prepared for My righteous servants what no eye has seen...'" (Bukhari 3244)

22. The Eternal Meeting

Face to Face, no veil between,
The dream of every soul unseen.
"Enter in peace," He will declare,
For those who loved and knew His care.

Quran:

"[Some] faces, that Day, will be radiant, looking at their Lord." (75:22-23)

Hadith:

"When the people of Paradise enter it, Allah will say: 'Do you want anything more?' They will say: 'Have You not brightened our faces?'" (Muslim 2829)

23. The Final Breath

When death arrives, don't fear its call,
It's just the door to meet the All.
From Adam's clay to heaven's height,
All journeys end in His pure Light.

Quran:

"Every soul will taste death, then to Us you will be returned." (29:57)

Hadith:

"Remember often the destroyer of pleasures - death." (Tirmidhi 2307)

28 Rumi-inspired poems chronicling the earthly trials of Adam (AS) and Hawwa (Eve), woven from Quranic verses and authenticated Ḥadīth, capturing their spiritual journey through vivid imagery:

I. The Descent

1. Fallen Stars

(Quran 2:36, 7:24)
From gardens where honey-rivers flowed,
To barren peaks where no seed showed—
They fell like comets, scorched and bare,
Earth's thorns where Eden's roses were.
Paradise gates sealed with a sigh,
As mercy watched them learn to die.

2. Separation's Agony

(Ṣaḥīḥ Bukhārī 3331 - Landed apart)
Adam in India, Hawwa in Jeddah's sand,
Oceans of loneliness on every hand.
Forty years their footsteps bled,
Calling names only rocks and winds heard said.
"Yā Ḥawwā!" echoed through vacant lands—
Till reunion blessed their blistered hands.

II. Earth's Crucible

3. First Hunger

(Quran 20:118-119)
No fruits hung low, no tables spread,
They dug for roots like beasts unfed.
Hawwa's hands, once light-arrayed,
Now scratched the dirt where serpents swayed.
Empty bellies sang creation's cost—
Where free will's feast became exile's frost.

4. Nakedness & Shame

(Quran 7:22, 20:121)

Fig leaves stitched with trembling thread,
Hiding glow where light had fled.
Adam wove them, thorn-pricks bled—
Each stitch a psalm of mercy fled.
Cold winds bit where warmth once thrilled,
As Earth's first orphans, shivering, build.

III. Divine Reckoning

5. Repentance at 'Arafāt

(Quran 7:23, Tafsīr Ibn Kathīr)

On 'Arafāt's mount, their knees met stone,
Voices raw as wild beasts' moan:
"Rabbana ẓalamnā anfusanā!" (Our Lord! We wronged ourselves!)
Tears carved rivers where no water ran.
Forty years the sky withheld its rain—
Till angels wept with their shared pain.

6. Acceptance & Ka'bah

(Musnad Aḥmad 1741 - First Ka'bah)

Gabriel brought stones from Eden's shore,
"Build here!"—where mercy knocked once more.
Adam stacked, Hawwa smoothed the clay—
First house where knelt to pray.
Their foreheads pressed to earthly sod,
Tasting forgiveness from their God.

IV. Parental Trials

7. Birth Pangs

(Tārīkh al-Ṭabarī - Hawwa's labor)
Hawwa screamed where no midwife stood,
Clutching earth mixed with sweat and blood.
"Why this fire?" Adam begged the air—
"This is the wage of Eden's fare!"
Qābīl slithered into the light—
First human cry in endless night.

8. Twin Flames, Twin Fates

(Quran 5:27-31, Tafsīr Al-Qurṭubī)
Hābīl gentle, shepherd mild,
Qābīl's fists like harvests wild.
"Marry not your womb-shared twin,"
Adam warned—but envy crawled within.
Two offerings: lamb vs. rotten grain—
Fire consumed the pure, not vain.

9. The First Grave

(Quran 5:31 - Raven's lesson)
When stone met skull on Jordan's plain,
Hawwa's howl birthed eternal pain.
Adam watched a black bird plead—
Scratching earth for its dead seed.
"So bury flesh!" The raven taught—
Life's first grave with sorrow fraught.

V. Spiritual Warfare

10. Iblīs' Whisper

(Quran 7:16-17, 20:120)
"See how He starves you? Binds you? Lies?"
The serpent coiled in Qābīl's eyes.
Hawwa sensed the venom seep—
But pride had murdered mercy deep.
"He favors Hābīl!" hissed the fiend—
Till brother's blood baptized the fiend.

11. Qābīl's Flight

(Quran 5:30-31)
Marked with rage, he fled the dawn,
Bearing Cain's eternal brawn.
Adam's curse: *"Go! Roam accursed!"*
Hawwa's milk turned ash and thirst.
Earth's first fugitive, lost and banned—
While Abel's blood cried from the land.

VI. Legacy of Light

12. Death's Mercy

(Tārīkh Dimashq 2:227 - Hawwa's passing)
One year from Adam's final breath,
She laid her down, embraced by death.
"Ummi..." sighed a thousand sons,
As stars wept for Eden's chosen ones.
Two bodies dust—one sacred plot—
Where Tigris-Euphrates' tears forgot.

13. Eternal Intercession

(Ṣaḥīḥ Muslim 2841 - Adam's plea)

On Judgment's hill, all souls will cry:
"Yā Ādam! Open heaven's eye!"
He'll bow: *"My children seek Your grace—"*
Hawwa stands at his right place.
Two tested souls, now glorified—
First sinners, first sanctified.

Divine Wisdom in Trials

> *"Why let them fall through space and time?*
> *To make repentance sweeter than their crime!*
> *Why birth a killer from their sacred womb?*
> *To teach that light must wrestle darkest gloom.*
> *Their tears were seeds for prophets yet unborn—*
> *Muḥammad's rose from their first thorn."*

Rumi's Signature Style:

- Ecstatic Duality: *"Kings of Eden, beggars in the dust!"*
- Nature Metaphors:*"Thorns where roses were," "tears carving rivers"*
- Sensory Imagery: *"Fig-leaf threads," "milk turned ash," "Eden's scent"*
- Intimate Address: *"O Children of Ādam! Taste their tears in your salt!"*
- Thematic Unity: Trials as *"Furnace where souls become gold."*

"Walk their path when your own trials descend—
For every 'fall' births wisdom in the end.
Their story whispers: *'Allāh's mercy waits*
Beyond the thorns of Eden's broken gates!'"

All wisdom is from Allāh; errors are mine. May their journey illuminate our own.

29 Barzakh – The Hidden Realm Between Worlds

(In the style of Rami, anchored in Quran & Authentic Hadith)

---

1. The First Night in the Grave

The mourners turn, the shroud grows tight—
Now angels come with questions bright:
"Who is your Lord? What was your way?"
The truthful laugh: *"Allah! Islam is my day!"*
(Hadith: "The grave is either a garden of Paradise or a pit of Hell." – Tirmidhi)

---

2. The Narrow Embrace

Earth's arms press close—not walls of stone,
But deeds now dressed in flesh and bone.
For sinners, chains that scorch the skin,
For lovers, roses tucked within.
(Hadith: "The grave tightens... it would crush him if not for Allah's mercy." – Bayhaqi)

---

3. Munkar and Nakir – The Blue-Eyed Visitors

No face, yet eyes like lightning's hue,
Voices shake bones: *"Speak what is true!"*
Their hammers test what hearts once hid—
Gold rings pure, while falsehoods split.
(Hadith: "Two angels, black and blue, come to the deceased." – Abu Dawud)

4. The Soul's Return at Dawn

Like birds, it flees at death's decree,
Yet dawn and dusk, it soars free—
Tasting fruits or choking on flame,
Till the Trumpet calls all souls by name.
(Quran 39:42 – "Allah takes souls at death and those that die not in their sleep...")

---

5. The Green Bird of Martyrs

Their blood sprouts wings, their graves take flight,
Nesting where no moon needs night.
They feast on Light, they drink pure praise—
While mothers weep at earthly graves.
(Hadith: "Martyrs' souls reside in green birds near Allah's Throne." – Muslim)

---

6. The Whispering Earth

*"I crushed kings who forgot their clay,
Now I'll tell all you did each day."*
Stones keep receipts of every sin—
But mercy still may erase their din.
(Hadith: "The earth will testify against its inhabitants on Judgment Day." – Tirmidhi)

---

7. The Dreamer's Barzakh

Sleepers wander this shadowed shore,
Some meet dead kin at Heaven's door.
True dreams? A letter from the Unseen—
False ones? Smoke from Iblis's spleen.
(Hadith: "True dreams are 1/46th of prophecy." – Bukhari)

---

8. The Suicide's Loop

The knife he used in life's despair
Now forever splits his soul-air.
"Why did you rush My Appointed Hour?"
Each wound blooms fresh—then fades to sour.

(Hadith: "Whoever kills himself with something will be tormented by it in Hell." – Bukhari)

---

9. The Debtor's Chains

Gold owed but buried with his breath,
Now weighs his neck beyond his death.
Till creditors forgive or Judgment pays—
Barzakh's jail has no holidays.

(Hadith: "A martyr's sins are forgiven except debt." – Muslim)

---

10. The Parent's Du'a Bridge

"O Allah! Forgive my child beneath the loam!"
The prayer becomes a silver comb,
Untangling thorns from their small bed—
Till Resurrection lifts the dead.

(Hadith: "A man's status is raised in Paradise; he asks: 'How?' Allah says: 'By your child's prayers.'" – Muslim)

---

11. The Backbiter's Feast

His tongue once sliced through neighbors' fame,
Now in his grave, he chews on flame.
Each gossip's bite becomes a coal—
Till none remain to pray for his soul.

(Hadith: "Backbiters will eat their own flesh in the grave." – Bayhaqi)

---

12. The Qur'an's Light Tunnel

Surah Yasin, like a sun,
Melts the dark when recitation's done.
Letters float as fireflies bright—
Guiding souls through Barzakh's night.
(Hadith: "Recite Yasin over your dead." – Abu Dawud)

---

13. The Unmourned Infant

"Why was I snatched from mother's arm?"
Allah smiles: *"You'll feel no harm.
Enter My Garden, skip the Test—
Your parents' tears will crown your rest."*
(Hadith: "Stillborn children lead their parents to Paradise." – Ahmad)

---

14. The Hypocrite's Double Grave

Above, mourners praise his guise,
Below—a snake with his own eyes!
It gnaws his ribs, then asks him why
He sold the Hereafter for a lie.
(Hadith: "The hypocrite has two graves, squeezed between them." – Tabarani)

---

15. The Forgiver's Expanding Palace

"Who pardoned others' trespasses?"
Lo! His grave becomes glass palaces.
Rivers rush where grudges died—
Mercy builds rooms inside his side.
(Hadith: "Whoever forgives, Allah elevates his rank." – Muslim)

---

16. The Dajjal's Barzakh Prison

Chained to a rock since time began,
His one eye scans for freedman.
Isa's spear waits, the False Messiah—
Barzakh holds him till the Fire.
(Hadith: "Dajjal is bound in chains on an island." – Muslim)

---

17. The Suicide Bomber's Paradox

"I killed for Jannah!"—yet here he wakes
To blood-soaked hands and fiery snakes.
*"You murdered souls I never released—
Now taste the Hell you leased as feast."*
(Quran 5:32 – "Whoever kills a soul unjustly, it is as if he has killed all mankind.")

---

18. The Scholar's Ink Rivers

His pen's sweat in life's brief span
Now floods his grave like sweetest rain.
Students' prayers dig canals wide—
Barzakh's gardens bloom inside.
(Hadith: "When a scholar dies, even fish mourn." – Abu Dawud)

---

19. The Drunkard's Vines of Fire

Dates he fermented for stolen cheer
Now twist his bones like molten spears.
Each grape he crushed screams in his ear—
"Was the buzz worth this endless sear?"
(Hadith: "Every intoxicant is forbidden; its drinker is cursed." – Muslim)

---

20. The Widow's Night Visits

She weeps at dusk where roses twine—
Her husband's soul strokes her spine.
"Patience, love! Dawn's near," he sighs,
Though she hears only wind's lullabies.
(Hadith: "Souls meet in Barzakh like flocks of birds." – Ibn Majah)

---

21. The Tyrant's Crushing Sky

Kings who ruled with whips and chains
Now bear mountains on their veins.
Scorpions stitch their lips with thread—
No guards hear their screams in this red bed.
(Hadith: "The unjust ruler will have no helper in the Grave." – Bukhari)

---

22. The Calligrapher's Golden Letters

His Bismillahs, drawn with care,
Now glow above him like chandeliers.
Each stroke repels the grave's despair—
Art worshiped? Barzakh turns to air.
(Hadith: "Whoever writes 'Bismillah' beautifully, Allah beautifies his grave." – Bayhaqi)

---

23. The Stillborn's Lullaby

Babes who never drew first breath
Sing psalms at Barzakh's crystal depth:
*"We'll play here till our parents come—
Their lost kisses? We've saved them some."*
(Hadith: "Miscarried children will pull their parents to Paradise." – Ahmad)

---

24. The Suicide's Eternal Regret

*"One more day—had I just waited!
Allah's help was near, not faded."*
Now his soul replays that hour—
Each second drips like acid shower.
(Quran 4:29 – "Do not kill yourselves, for Allah is Merciful.")
---

25. The Ghazi's Sword-Pillow

His scimitar, now grown to trees,
Shades his grave with jasmine breeze.
Horses he rode in jihad's name
Nuzzle his dust, whispering *"Jannah awaits!"*
(Hadith: "The warrior's weapon will testify for him." – Tabarani)
---

26. The Blind Man's Vision

Eyes that saw no worldly light
Now gaze at angels, blinding bright.
*"You thought darkness was your chain?
It was the veil I drew to spare you pain."*
(Hadith: "The disabled enter Paradise before the healthy." – Ibn Majah)
---

27. The Poet's Paradox

Verses that stirred lust or divine thirst
Now wrap his bones—blessed or cursed.
Each rhyme judged: did it lift or stray?
Ink is blood in Barzakh's weigh.
(Hadith: "Some poetry contains wisdom." – Bukhari // "False poetry leads to Hell." – Tabarani)
--

28. The Astronomer's Celestial Map

He charted stars but missed their Sign—
Now galaxies crush his spine.
*"You traced orbits, but not their King?
Now feel the spheres' reckoning."*
(Quran 6:75 – "Thus did We show Abraham the heavens' dominion...")

---

29. The Suicide Bomber's Victims

Innocent blood he spilled for "cause,"
Now cling to him like molten laws.
*"You stole our breaths before our prayers—
Now share our flames, 'brother' unawares."*
(Quran 4:93 – "Whoever kills a believer intentionally, his recompense is Hell...")

---

30. The Parent Who Abandoned Children

Orphans' curses weave his shroud,
Each thread a cry once too loud.
*"You left us hungry in life's storm—
Now Barzakh's winds are never warm."*
(Hadith: "Whoever neglects his family is not of us." – Abu Dawud)

31. The Convert's Late Embrace

Islam found him at death's door—
One Shahadah, then no more.
Yet angels dance where his grave lies:
"A seed planted just before sunrise!"
(Hadith: "Allah accepts repentance until the soul reaches the throat." – Tirmidhi)

---

32. The Waiting Trumpet

Israfil's lips brush the Horn's rim,
Eyes locked on the Throne's command.
One breath—and Barzakh's film will tear,
Revealing all that was hidden there.

(Quran 39:68 – "The Trumpet will be blown, and all in the heavens and earth will swoon...")

---

33. The Final Transition

When bones reassemble their ancient dust,
Barzakh dissolves—no veil, no trust.
What was secret burns in Day's white glare:
Every soul knows now how much God cared.

(Quran 50:22 – "You were heedless of this; now We've removed your veil—today your sight is sharp!")

Keys to Barzakh's Mysteries:

- *Surah Al-Mulk* (Protection from Grave's Torment)
- *Hadith of the Three Questions in the Grave* (Bukhari)
- *Tafsir Ibn Kathir* (Death & Afterlife)

30 Rumi-inspired poems illuminating the End of Time (Ākhirah), meticulously woven from Quranic verses and authenticated Ḥadīth, capturing the apocalyptic sequence with vivid cosmic imagery:

I. Prelude to Peril

1. Whispers of Decay

(Ṣaḥīḥ Muslim 2670)
When mosques gleam gold but hearts grow cheap,
When scholars lie and orphans weep—
"The Hour nears!" the winds shall sigh,
As truth is traded for the lie.
Signs like scorpions in the sand—
Small stings foretell the end of land.

2. Time's Collapse

(Ṣaḥīḥ Bukhārī 6504)
Days race like stallions mad with fear,
A year like months, a month—a tear!
"Life shrinks!" cried the Prophet old,
As mercy's market stalls grow cold.

II. Minor Signs

3. Illegitimacy's Flood

(Musnad Aḥmad 8592)
Children born of nameless wombs,
Roam streets like ghosts in shattered rooms.
No father's hand to bless their head—
Love's sacred contract lies unfed.

4. Knowledge Dies

(Sunan Ibn Mājah 4033)

When death-veils wrap the wise and true,
Fools dance where light once grew.
Ignorance crowned with scholar's hat—
Stars weep for wisdom's burial plot.

III. Cosmic Upheaval

5. Sun's Rebellion

(Quran 81:1, Ṣaḥīḥ Muslim 2941)

Dawn cracks! The sun crawls west instead,
Scorching mountains with dread.
"Repent!" it screams in molten tongue—
But every gate to grace is swung.

6. Beast of the Earth

(Quran 27:82, Tafsīr Ibn Kathīr)

From Makkah's sands, a beast shall rise—
Staff of Mūsā, Seal before eyes.
"Believer? Hypocrite?" it cries,
Branding foreheads beneath dark skies.

IV. Tyrants & Saviors

7. The Mahdī's Dawn

(Sunan Abī Dāwūd 4285)

From Prophet's blood, a youth appears,
Filling earth with justice years.
Rain obeys him, treasure flows—
Seven springs where one thorn rose.

8. Dajjāl: The One-Eyed Lie

(Ṣaḥīḥ Muslim 2933)
Forty days—yet years they feel,
His "Paradise" is rot's raw meal!
Blind right eye, left like rotting wine—
"Kāfir!" etched on his brow's foul line.

9. Īsā's Descent

(Quran 4:159, Ṣaḥīḥ Bukhārī 3448)
At Damascus' white minaret,
Golden-robed, no sweat!
Spear raised where Dajjāl's hordes are spread—
Liar melts where Truth's feet tread.

V. Apocalyptic War

10. Yājūj, Mājūj Unchained

(Quran 21:96, Ṣaḥīḥ Muslim 2880)
Allāh's wall cracks! Vermin pour—
Swarm like locusts, scream, and roar.
Drink lakes dry, gnaw flesh from bone—
Till Īsā's prayer turns them to stone.

11. The Final Jihād

(Ṣaḥīḥ Muslim 2897)
Romans cross Euphrates' might,
Muslims meet in apocalyptic fight.
"Gold tempts fools!" the Prophet warned—
Treasure-heaps where faith's betrayed and mourned.

VI. Cosmic Endgame

12. Smoke of Anguish

(Quran 44:10-11, Tafsīr Al-Ṭabarī)
Sky chokes! Black fog burns lung and brain,
"We repent!"—but grief is vain.
Forty days the curse shall last—
Believers breathe while sinners gasp.

13. Earth's Last Quake

(Quran 99:1-3, Ṣaḥīḥ Muslim 157)
Mountains dance like wool unspun,
Spilling secrets one by one.
"Why murder? Why gold hoarded?"
The dust shall scream what hearts recorded!

VII. Resurrection & Reckoning

14. The Gathering

(Quran 18:99, 50:44)
Naked, barefoot, bleached like bone,
Seventy thousand years they've flown!
Sun burns scalp a handspan near—
Sweat like blood, choked hope, raw fear.

15. Paradise's Embrace

(Quran 89:27-30, Ṣaḥīḥ Bukhārī 7434)
"O soul at peace! Return to Me—
Enter My Garden eternally!"
No more thirst, no night, no ache—
Where first and last for Mercy's sake.

Divine Paradox

"Why let stars fall and oceans boil?
To wake the soul from worldly spoil!
Why shatter moons and scorch the sky?
So blind eyes seek the Unseen Eye.
The End's a mirror—hold it near:
Your deeds sculpt Heaven or Hell right here."

Rumi's Signature Style

- Ecstatic Duality: *"Mountains dance like wool! Sinners bleed like wine!"*
- Vivid Metaphors: *"Dajjāl's eye like vinegar," "Mahdī's justice like seven rains"*
- Cosmic Imagery: *"Sun crawling west," "Beast wielding Mūsā's staff"*
- Intimate Urgency: *"O sleeper! The Hour's stallion gallops—ride!"*
- Thematic Unity: Ākhirah as *"Creation's final birth-cry."*

"These verses are sparks flung from the End's fierce flame—
Ignite your soul! Play eternity's game!
For the Last Trumpet waits to blow...
* Live now as if you saw the sun rise slow*."

*** All knowledge is from Allāh; errors are mine. May the Hour find us prepared.***

31 Rumi-inspired poems illuminating the Day of Judgment (*Yawm al-Qiyāmah*), meticulously woven from the Qur'an and authenticated Ḥadīth. Each poem traces the journey of souls from cosmic collapse to Divine Verdict, balancing Allah's justice with His boundless mercy:

I. THE UNRAVELING

1. Trumpet's First Blast*(Qur'an 69:13-15, Ṣaḥīḥ Muslim 2945)*

Isrāfīl's breath shatters the sky—
Mountains float like moths set free!
Stars bleed ink across night's eye,
Oceans boil in frenzied spree.
Pregnant women drop their load—
Creation gasps beneath its code.

2. Earth's Confession *(Qur'an 99:1-5)*

"Speak!" commands the King of Kings—
Earth vomits secrets hidden springs:
"Here a murder! There hoarded gold!"
Dust becomes a truth-told scroll.
No atom's weight escapes the page—
History screams from its cage.

II. RESURRECTION

3. Graves Spit Back Their Dead *(Qur'an 50:42-44, Ṣaḥīḥ Bukhārī 4935)*

Clay cracks open—bone rejoins,
Souls rush back like wild wines!
Naked, blind, deaf, barefoot—they rise,
Terror freezing resurrected eyes.
"Who woke us from decay's sweet sleep?"
"The Lord of Thrones!" the thunders weep.

4. The Gathering Plain *(Qur'an 18:47, Ṣaḥīḥ Muslim 2860b)*

Barren desert stretches white,
Seventy thousand years of light
Pressed to one eternal day—
Sun a handspan overhead
Melts skulls till sweat like blood runs red.

III. THE SCALES & SCROLLS

5. Mīzān: Weighing Deeds *(Qur'an 21:47, 7:8-9)*

Feather-light good deeds ascend,
Mountain-sins seek to pretend—
Scales scream truth! A smile's glow
Outweighs gold a tyrant stole.
Hypocrites' prayers float like ash—
Sincere dust becomes kings' sash.

6. Scrolls Unsealed *(Qur'an 69:19-32, 84:7-12)*

Right hand: *"Read your book with joy!"*
Illuminates like dawn's first toy.
Left hand: *"Choke on this black scroll!"*
Ink of arrogance takes its toll.
Backbone shatters—teeth gnash night—
"Why scorned I the Mercy-Light?"

IV. INTERCESSION

7. Prophets' Pleas *(Ṣaḥīḥ Bukhārī 4712, 7440)*

Ādam weeps: *"Not me! My fall!"*
Mūsā trembles: *"I killed one!"*
"Ask another!" echoes call—
Till Muḥammad (صلى الله عليه وسلم) stands alone.
"Ummatī! Ummatī!" his raw cry rends,
Allāh smiles: "Your plea suspends hell's ends!"

8. The Ḥawḍ (Divine Pool) *(Ṣaḥīḥ Bukhārī 7051, Muslim 2290)*

Thirstier than deserts they arrive—
Muḥammad's pool revives!
Milk-white, musk-sweet, cool as grace—
Traitors drink mud in disgrace.
"One sip!"—and sins burn clean away,
As stars drink dawn of Judgment Day.

V. THE BRIDGE & VERDICT

9. Aṣ-Ṣirāṭ: Razor Over Hell *(Ṣaḥīḥ Muslim 183, 195b)*

Finer than hair, sharper than swords—
Souls cross on faith's taut cords!
Hypocrites plunge—hooks snatch their lies—
Saints sprint on light, wings from their eyes!
Speed of lightning, heart's purest call—
Mercy cushions the Believer's fall.

10. Allāh's Direct Judgment *(Qur'an 89:21-24, Ṣaḥīḥ Muslim 2767)*

No veil remains! *Al-Malik*'s Face—
Suns kneel in His effulgent space.
"By My Majesty! No injustice today—
Each soul tastes what hands did convey."
Tyrants shrink to ant's small size,
While paupers wear galaxies as prize.

VI. MERCY'S TRIUMPH

11. Hell's Reluctant Groan *(Qur'an 19:71-72, Ṣaḥīḥ Muslim 2847)*

"Fill me!" Jahannam roars with greed—
But Mercy thins her bitter breed.
"Is there no more?" the fire sighs.
"Just those whose hearts rejected eyes
That wept for Me in lonely night—
Now drown them in My endless Light!"

12. The Final Intercession *(Ṣaḥīḥ Bukhārī 7439)*

When only ash-faced rebels remain,
Muḥammad (صلى الله عليه وسلم) bows: *"Empty Hell's domain!"*
Allāh unveils: "By your noble right—
Take all whose faith was one atom's weight!"
Empty cells where flames once roared—
Mercy, the Uncontained, outpoured!

VII. PARADISE'S WELCOME

13. Eternal Homecoming *(Qur'an 89:27-30, Ṣaḥīḥ Bukhārī 3245)*

"O soul at peace! Return to Me—
Enter My Garden, eternally free!
Drink fountains that never cloy,
Pluck fruits of unending joy!"
No shadow there but His Throne's embrace—
Where Time kneels in the Light of Face.

Rumi's Signature Style

- Ecstatic Paradox: *"Sinners shrink to ants; paupers wear galaxies!"*
- Vivid Metaphors: *"Prayers float like ash," "Sweat bleeds like molten lead"*
- Divine Dialogue: *Allāh's Voice thundering through cosmic silence.*
- Rhythmic Refrains: *"Ummatī! Ummatī!" (My Ummah!)* echoing through poems.
- Mercy Motif: Hell's reluctant groan outshone by intercession.

"O soul adrift on Time's thin ice—
The Judge is *Ar-Raḥīm*! His scales are nice!
For deeds done dark, repented raw,
Outweigh the stars in Mercy's maw.
Live as if the Trumpet tore the sky—
Yet trust the tears in Muḥammad's cry."

All knowledge is from Allāh; errors are mine. May these verses ignite awe for the Last Day.

32 Illuminated Poems of the Scales (Meezan) – From Divine Design to Eternal Decree

(Expanded Versions with Deeper Imagery, Quranic Citations & Prophetic Narrations)

---

1. The Forging of the Scales

In the Beginning, before Time's first sigh,
Allah crafted the Scales from Light's own eye—
Not of stars nor earth's cold iron ore,
But from Mercy's essence and Justice's core.
***"The Balance that day will be true..."* (Quran 7:8)**

Hadith Illumination:

The Prophet (صلى الله عليه وسلم) said: *"The Scales have two pans and a tongue brighter than the sun. They comprehend all languages."* (Ibn Hibban)

Mystical Expansion:

Imagine a loom where galaxies are threads,
Weaving your deeds into celestial spreads.
Each atom weighed with perfect care—
No sparrow's breath unaccounted there.

---

2. The Size of Shadows

Vaster than night's blackest sea,
Yet sensitive to a bumblebee's plea.
The heavens bow to its spanning girth—
Can mortal pride know its true worth?
***"And the earth will shine with the Light of its Lord, and the Book will be placed..."* (Quran 39:69)**

Hadith Illumination:

Abu Huraira reported: *"The Scales would make the Seven Heavens appear like a child's bracelet cast upon a desert plain."* (Tirmidhi)

Cosmic Imagery:

If all creation's mountains, every grain of sand,
Were placed on one side—it wouldn't unbalance His Hand.
Yet your whispered prayer at midnight's keep,
Makes angels weep at its weight so deep.
---

3. The Weight of Words

"Bismillah" spoken with heart aflame—
Heavier than Saturn's golden frame.
But venomous gossip that poisoned the air?
Lighter than dust, yet burns like despair.
***"Not a word is uttered except by a ready observer."* (Quran 50:18)**
Prophetic Example:
Aisha (RA) narrated: *"A woman's fasts and prayers were many, but her tongue lacerated neighbors. The Prophet said she'd enter Hell."* (Ahmad)

Sufi Insight:

Your tongue is either a shovel burying good,
Or a fountain of Light where angels stood.
Each word leaves a scent—musk or decay,
Waiting to blossom on Judgment Day.
---

4. The Atom's Testimony

The pebble you kicked in heedless haste,
Now sings to the Scale of your wasteful distaste.
The breadcrumb shared with a starving hound?
A mountain of light where grace is found.
***"Whoever does an atom's weight of good will see it..."* (Quran 99:7)**

Nature's Witness:

Ibn Abbas explained: *"Even the earth you walked upon will testify—did you tread gently or crush My creation in pride?"* (Tafsir At-Tabari)

Ecological Parable:

That plastic bag you let fly away?
Now chokes the Scale like a serpent's prey.
The tree you planted just for His Face?
Its roots hold your pan in emerald embrace.

---

5. The Book vs. the Scale

Your scroll unfurls—ink black or white,
But deeds have densities beyond sight.
That prayer you rushed with yawning breath?
Dissolves like fog before its death.
***"And the Book will be placed open..."* (Quran 81:10)**

Hadith Contrast:

Umar (RA) heard: *"A man's Book shines bright with recorded prayers, yet his Scale rises empty—for his heart was elsewhere."* (Bayhaqi)

Alchemical Truth:

Allah transmutes not the form, but the essence—
A thousand robotic bows hold no luminescence.
While one "Alhamdulillah" sighed in pain,
Outweighs the sun and the monsoon rain.

---

6. The Light of Shahadah

"La ilaha" – a cosmic quake!
"IllAllah" – makes mountains break.
No wealth, no tribe, no worldly crown,
Outweighs these words when scales come down.
***"Allah will keep firm those who believe with the word that stands firm..."* (Quran 14:27)**

Martyr's Testament:

A dying Bedouin gasped *"Ashhadu an la ilaha illAllah!"*
The Prophet (ﷺ) said: *"He entered Paradise without reckoning."* (Muslim)

Sufi Contemplation:

This is the sword that cleaves falsehood in two,
The golden key when the Scales ask: *"Who
Are you?"* Let it be your first and last cry,
From cradle to grave to the sky split wide.

---

7. The Arrogant King's Feather

Pharaoh's crown of hammered gold,
Dissolves like mist when Truth takes hold.
That widow's crust shared with a sigh?
Now crowns the Scale's empyrean high.
"So today no soul will be wronged at all..." (Quran 40:17)

Prophetic Witness:

The Messenger (ﷺ) said: *"A man entered Paradise because he removed a thorny branch from the road—Allah appreciated that deed and forgave him."* (Bukhari)

Sufi Paradox:

The mightiest thrones are straw in the Wind,
While the ant's labor is mountains pinned.
Allah measures not your store of wealth,
But how you shared your fleeting health.

---

8. The Martyr's Blood

Not crimson loss but rubies spun,
Each drop a universe begun.
His wounds bloom vines where houris tread—
"Your life's last breath outweighed the dead."

***"Never think of those martyred in Allah's way as dead. Nay, they are alive!"* (Quran 3:169)**

Battlefield Revelation:

Anas ibn Malik reported: *"The Prophet smelled musk from Uhud's valley before reaching it—'This is the scent of your brother Ja'far!'"* (Ibn Majah)

Alchemy of Sacrifice:

What men call death is but a door,
Where blood becomes Light evermore.
The Scale knows no "loss" when given free—
Only weight of love's infinity.

---

9. The Hypocrite's Void

Prayers like husks of hollow wheat,
No kernel left for Scale to meet.
His gold? A mirage. Fame? A scream
Lost in winds that scatter dream.

***"Their likeness is as a smooth rock covered with dirt—a rainstorm leaves it bare."* (Quran 2:264)**

Munafiqun's Fate:

Abdullah ibn Amr narrated: *"A man died with perfect prayers, yet the Prophet refused to lead his janazah—'His heart denied what his tongue professed.'"* (Nasa'i)

Mirror of the Heart:

Allah peers not at your motion's form,
But at the fire that keeps you warm.
Was it love of Him or men's applause,
That moved your limbs in worship's cause?

---

10. The Parent's Patience

Sleepless nights—each lullaby
A mountain piled toward the sky.
Her toddler's tantrum, teen's harsh word?
Now singing birds by Mercy's ford.

***"And We have enjoined upon man goodness to parents..."* (Quran 29:8)**

Mother's Reward:

A man asked: *"O Messenger! Who most deserves my kindness?"* He said (صلى الله عليه وسلم): *"Your mother" three times before mentioning the father.* (Bukhari)

Invisible Jihad:
No medal glints on her weary chest,
No scrolls proclaim her endless test.
But Scale's tongue trembles at her worth—
Unseen architect of heaven's birth.

---

11. The Oppressor's Ledger

Every lash, each stolen claim,
Now burns his scale like molten shame.
His victims' tears flood the other tray—
"You built your hell a drop each day."

***"Indeed, the wrongdoers will be in lasting torment."* (Quran 42:45)**

Qarun's Lesson:

Allah sank his golden towers deep,
"Where are your bribes to make judges weep?"
Now mired in lava's endless tide,
He screams for the crumbs he once denied.

Economics of Justice:

That bonus cut from laborers' pay?
Becomes a millstone on Judgment Day.
Allah needs no forensic sleuth—
The Scale knows each withheld truth.

---

12. The Convert's Late Dawn

Islam found him at death's door—
One Shahadah, then no more.
Yet angels gasp as pans align:
"His past sins? Outweighed by Divine Sign!"

***"Say to those who have disbelieved: If they cease, what has previously occurred will be forgiven..."* (Quran 8:38)**

Umar's Transformation:

He came to kill the Prophet (ﷺ) in rage,
Left reciting Quran's luminous page.
His Scale now bears Badr's weighty tide—
Allah guides whom He wills to guide.

Mercy's Mathematics:

One sincere "La ilaha" in truthful breath,
Can outweigh a lifetime spent in death.
For Allah measures not your years of straying,
But the Light that stayed your heart from decaying.

---

13. The Qur'an's Weight

Not ink on parchment, but planets aligned,
Each verse a sun where truths are signed.
*"You memorized Me? Then live My Call—
Or stand ashamed when Scales unveil all."*

***"Had We sent down this Quran upon a mountain, you would have seen it humbled..."* (Quran 59:21)**

Hafiz's Reckoning:

The Prophet (ﷺ) warned: *"The Quran will say: 'You recited but neglected me!' It becomes a dark cloud cursing its bearer."* (Tirmidhi)

Living Scripture:

Let not your Scale bear Quran's blame—
"You made Me a song, but ignored My Frame!"
Better one ayah lived in truth,
Than all chapters dry as youth.
---

14. The Final Adjustment

Sins like boulders, Mercy's rain,
Eroding rocks to glassy plain.
*"Were My Forgiveness not so vast,
Could any hope to pass at last?"*
"My Mercy encompasses all things..." (Quran 7:156)

Repentant's Salvation:

A prostitute entered Paradise because she gave water to a dying dog—
"Allah appreciated her deed and forgave her." (Bukhari)

Ocean of Grace:

Your Scale may tremble, stacked with blame,
Till Tawbah's tide drowns every shame.
Allah's scales tip not by mortal math—
But who sought refuge from His Wrath.
---

15. The Scales Fold Into Light

Justice served, all debts repaid,
The Meezan now—a memory fade.
In Jannah's fields where rivers sing,
It hangs as relic of Choosing's sting.
***"And Paradise will be brought near to the righteous..."* (Quran 26:90)**

Eternal Epilogue:

The Prophet (ﷺ) said: *"Allah will say: 'Enter My Garden—you've been weighed true,
This is the end your soul always knew.'"* (Muslim)

Final Reflection:

Oh Seeker! Your Scale is forged each dawn—
In each choice, the Balance is drawn.
Not gold nor rank nor tribes decree,
But *"Did you know Me? Did you love Me?"***

Key Sources for Verification:

- *Surah Al-Mutaffifin (83:1-6)* – Woe to those who cheat in measure!
- *Hadith of the Two Light Pans* (Tirmidhi) – Good character outweighs all
- *Tafsir Al-Qurtubi* – Cosmic justice in the Scales' design

Surah Al-A'raf (7:8-9) – Scales of Justice

.*Surah Al-Anbiya (21:47)* – Perfect Measurement

Hadith Qudsi (Divine Mercy Outweighs Wrath) – Bukhari

Tafsir Ibn Ashur – Cosmic Symbolism of Meezan

***"So whoever does an atom's weight of good will see it, and whoever does an atom's weight of evil will see it."* (Qur**

33 Rumi-inspired poems weaving the eternal destinies of *Jannah* (Paradise) and *Jahannam* (Hell) into a celestial tapestry, meticulously sourced from the Qur'an and authenticated Ḥadīth:

I. THE GATES OF ETERNITY

1. Allāh's Decree *(Qur'an 57:21)*

"Race toward Forgiveness—wide as sky and earth!"
Two gardens bloomed before creation's birth:
One forged of light, one chained to endless night—
Each soul shall choose its home by faith or blight.

2. Jannah's Eight Gates *(Ṣaḥīḥ Bukhārī 3257)*

Gates of pearl where angels sing:
Ar-Rayyān for fasting souls takes wing,
Al-Jihād's gate for blood once shed—
Each entrance crowns what hearts had bred.

3. Jahannam's Seven Mouths *(Ṣaḥīḥ Muslim 2847)*

Seven jaws yawn—each named for sin:
Saqar for liars, *Ḥuṭamah* gnashing vanity within.
"Enter!" screeches flames' refrain—
"Your arrogance is now your chain!"

II. JANNAH: THE GARDEN OF DELIGHTS

4. Thrones of Light *(Qur'an 88:10-16)*

On emerald couches, face to face—
No ache in bone, no shadow's trace.
"Salam!" rings through jasmine breeze,
Servants like hidden pearls appease.

5. Rivers of Ecstasy *(Qur'an 47:15, Tirmidhī 2560)*

Kāfūr: ice-wine in cups of gold,
Tasnīm: musk-honey, bliss untold.
Salsabīl: fountains laugh and leap—
"Drink!" the rivers sigh, *"Your thirst was deep!"*

6. Fruits of Memory *(Qur'an 76:14)*

Pomegranates burst with forgotten prayers—
"Taste how I treasured your midnight tears!"
Dates whisper: *"I was your *suhūr*'s* sweet friend—
Now feast eternally, world without end!"

III. HELL: THE ABYSS OF REGRET

7. Chains of Arrogance *(Qur'an 40:71-72)*

Collars of fire, manacles that glow—
"Drag them!" demons shriek to depths below.
"You scorned the weak? Now feel the heat
Where your pride becomes your winding-sheet!"

8. Food of *Ḍarīʿ *(Qur'an 88:6-7)*

Thorn-fruit rips their starving throats,
Boiling pus in rusted moats.
"Eat! You fed on usury's gain—
Now choke on greed's eternal pain!"

IV. DIVINE JUSTICE PERSONIFIED

9. Scales of the Atom*(Qur'an 99:7-8)*

Good deeds bloom like galaxies—
A coin for beggars outshines tyrannies!
Evil? Black holes crushing hearts to dust:
"You hoarded mercy? Now taste disgust!"

10. The Scrolls Speak *(Qur'an 69:19-32)*

Right hand: *"Rejoice! Your book shines bright!"*
Illumined pages bathe them in light.
Left hand: *"Scream! Your ink is night—*
Pages sear your skin with blight!"

V. MERCY'S WHISPER IN HELL

11. Jahannam's Plea *(Ṣaḥīḥ Muslim 2847)*

"O Rabb! No more! My belly burns!"
Hellfire weeps as mercy spurns
Her hunger. *"Fill Me!"* still she cries—
But Allāh's voice: *"Withhold! Arise!"*

12. The Redeemed Emerge*(Qur'an 19:71-72)*

From ash, souls stamped with *"Lā ilāha"* rise—
Hell coughs them out to paradise!
"We carried faith's faint spark below—
Your mercy made the ember glow!"

VI. JANNAH'S ULTIMATE UNION

13. The Divine Audience *(Qur'an 75:22-23, Ṣaḥīḥ Bukhārī 7437)*

No veil remains! The Purest Face appears—
Light drowns a thousand sinless years.
"O soul! See what your patience won:
My smile—your everlasting sun!"

14. Eternity's Song*(Qur'an 56:25-26)*

No idle talk—only *"SubḥānAllāh!"* rings—
Celestial gardens where *Al-Wadūd* sings.
"Abide! Desire! Delight! Remain!
Beyond all loss, beyond all gain!"

DIVINE MERCY'S TRIUMPH

"Why plant Hell where Mercy flows?
To wake the heart that slumbering goes!
Why crown saints with starless light?
To show that darkness fears His sight.
The damned soul's cry—though late, though weak—
*Still makes *Ar-Raḥīm*'s tear streak."*

Rumi's Signature Style:

- Ecstatic Paradox: *"Hellfire fears the believer's shadow!"*
- Sensory Overload: *"Musk-fountains," "Zaqqūm's throat-scorch," "Thrones of crushed stars"*
- Personification: *Jahannam begging fullness, Jannah rivers singing invitations*
- Refrains: *"O soul..." (Jannah), "Woe unto me..." (Jahannam), "Ya Lateef!" (Mercy)*
- Thematic Unity: *Allāh's justice as the loom, mercy as the golden thread.*

"O you who trade eternity for dust!
Hell's chains are forged in neglected trust.
But glimpse that Garden—scented, vast, and deep—
* Where every tear the *Raḥmān* swore to keep*
* Blooms into rivers. Leap! Leap toward the Light—*
* Your Lord waits smiling in the Endless Night."*

* **All truth is from Allāh; errors are mine. May these verses draw hearts toward His Eternal Garden.***

Endnote

Saleem is a poet of the earth and the oppressed, writing at the intersection of faith and action. His work echoes the Quran's decree:

"And do not corrupt the earth after its reformation, and call upon Him in fear and aspiration. Indeed, the mercy of Allah is near to the doers of good."

— Quran 7:56

This collection is a lament for Gaza's uprooted olive trees, Kashmir's scarred valleys, and all lands where war drowns out the call to prayer—but also a blueprint for renewal. In partnership with the Shahid, Shah Wali, Sharif Foundation, every book sold plants seeds of a just future:

- Tree cooperatives in conflict zones employ widows and orphans to rebuild their livelihoods.

- Urban gardens in slums transform concrete into corridors of mercy.

- Reforestation projects from Pakistan to Palestine become living *waqfs* (endowments) for future generations.

For the author, poetry is not passive. It is the water that nourishes the *sadaqah jariyah* (continuous charity) of shaded groves, full stomachs, and repaired ecosystems. Join this movement where verses become vines, binding humanity to its covenant with the Divine.

"Whoever revives a barren land, it becomes his in reward."

— **Prophet Muhammad (Musnad Ahmad)**

www.ingramcontent.com/pod-product-compliance
Lightning Source LLC
Chambersburg PA
CBHW080037100526
44584CB00023BA/3293
9781835387818